*Only after the traveler
has stopped to reflect
has his real journey begun.*

—from T. Serstevens

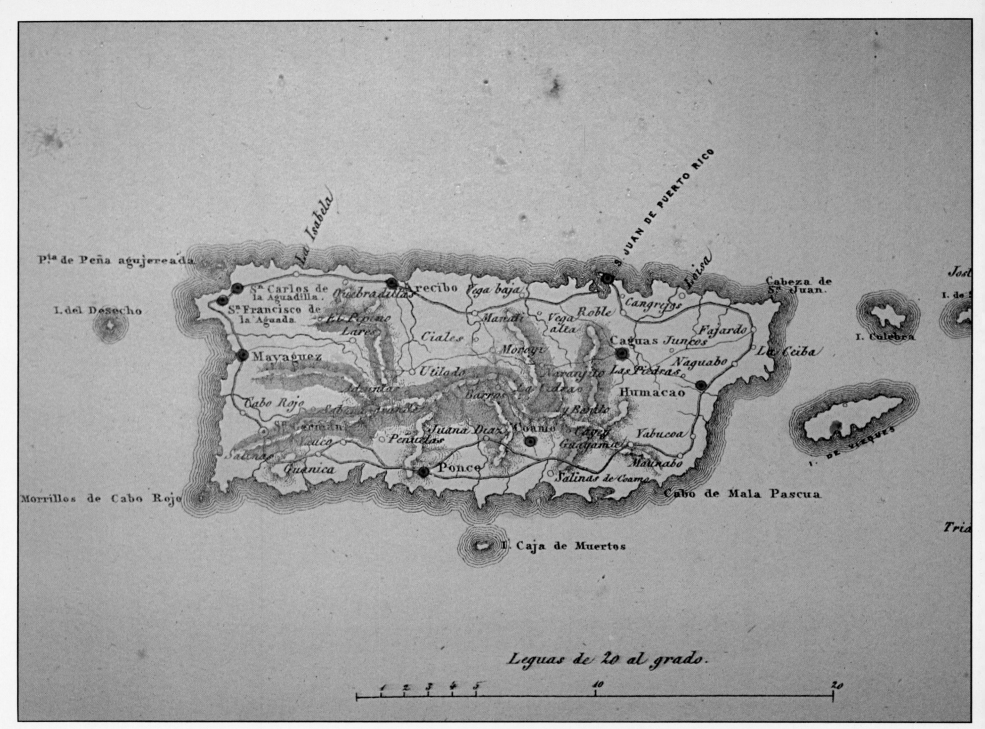

Pta de Peña agujereada

I. del Desecho

Morrillos de Cabo Rojo

Tria

Lat. Isabela

Sn Carlos de la Aguadilla
Sn Francisco de la Agua
El Pepino
Lares
Mayaguez
Cabo Rojo
Sabana grande
Sn German
Lauco
Salinas
Guanica

Arecibo
Quebradillas
Vega baja
Manati
Ciales
Utuado
Adjuntas
barros
Peñuelas
Juana Diaz
Ponce

SN JUAN DE PUERTO RICO

Vega alta
Roble
Monayi
Naranjito
La Cidra
y Bonito
Coamo
Salinas de Coamo

Cangrejos
Caguas Juncos
Las Piedras
Humacao
Cagey
Guayama
Yabucoa
Maunabo

Luisa

Cabeza de Sa Juan.
Fajardo
Naguabo
La Cciba

Cabo de Mala Pascua

Jost
I. de S

I. Colebra

I. DE VIEQUES

I. Caja de Muertos

Leguas de 20 al grado.

1 2 3 4 5   10   20

Antique map of Puerto Rico from a 19th-century atlas; courtesy Teodoro Vidal, San Juan.

*To Puerto Ricans everywhere
who cherish the heritage of their
beloved* Borinquen, *this book is
affectionately dedicated*

The setting sun adds a golden glow to the smile of seven-year-old Milagros Rivera, peeling an orange outside her home near Yabucoa. Blessed with a prosperity her grandparents could only have dreamed of, the questions posed for Milagros's future are those posed for all of Puerto Rico—how preserve the rising prosperity of the past few decades, all the while preserving the best of the country's heritage?

Images of Puerto Rico

Text and photographs by
Roger A. LaBrucherie

Imágenes Press

A rocky promontory is the lonely site of the Punta Tuna Light House, guardian of Puerto Rico's extreme southeastern corner for nearly a century. Part of a legacy of some four hundred years of Spanish rule over the island, the light house was built in 1892, near the end of Spain's last century of rule over the island, when increasing commercial activity on and around the island led to the construction of some 15 light houses to mark hazards to navigation and entrances to harbors. Today radio navigation increasingly replaces the role of the rotating beams, and sadly, many have been lost to the ravages of natural and human elements; but a few of the solitary sentinels still guide the island's coastal fishing vessels and other small boats, and continue to enhance the island's beauty and heritage.

Foreword

The seed of the idea which grew into Images of Puerto Rico was planted, I suppose, some fifteen years ago when I first came to Puerto Rico to undergo my training for service in the Peace Corps. Like many newcomers to Puerto Rico, my first exposure was to Viejo San Juan; unlike many visitors, however, I had the opportunity to get to know the other Puerto Rico—that is, the Puerto Rico outside San Juan—la isla, as Puerto Ricans call it. And over the ensuing years of occasional travels to and through Puerto Rico I became aware of the general public's lack of knowledge and understanding of the whole of Puerto Rico, in both the geographic and cultural senses. Thus it was that when I began some years ago to compile written and photographic observations about different lands, Puerto Rico was often in the back of my mind as the next project. I am happy to now be able to bring that long-held ambition to fruition.

Images of Puerto Rico is my fifth in a series of photographic-essay books on various places, all with a similar theme. I explained that theme in an earlier work, and I will use the same words here, for I find I can not improve upon them now: " . . . As with my previous books, this one is an attempt to capture the essence of a place and its people, primarily for the person who has had only a relatively brief time to spend there.

" . . . ever since I first lived abroad, well over a decade ago, I have been aware of the particular perspective and fresh insight a foreigner's eye can provide in looking at a country. Like a child, a newcomer is blessed with the ignorance that can lead to curiosity; from curiosity, to investigation; and from investigation, to understanding. It is that somewhat childlike curiosity, illuminated by understanding, that I have always tried to bring to my portrayal of

a country, and in that respect this book has much in common with its predecessors. In fact, I find that that fresh perspective is so quickly dulled that after even a few weeks 'covering' a country I frequently seek out tourists for the very purpose of once again trying to 'see' through their fresh eyes.

"It must be recognized that that special perspective does not come bias-free: a foreigner necessarily carries with him a set of values shaped by his own culture. Even were it remotely possible, I would not attempt to define all those values, but I feel I should comment on one: coming as I do from what is generally considered to be a 'developed' society, where a great deal is new, big, and impersonal, I am greatly captivated by those aspects of a country which are traditional, small and personal."

Thus, the reader should not be surprised to see a considerable emphasis in this book on the people of Puerto Rico and on the traditional aspects of her culture. While such a bias necessarily means slighting certain other aspects (there are relatively few photographs of the island's beaches and other tourist attractions, for example), I hope that this deficiency will be understood and accepted—especially in view of the ample coverage given those aspects by already-existing books about the island.

Anyone with an interest in Puerto Rico repeatedly encounters the assertion that the island has "a bad press," or "an image problem." If that allegation is true, I believe it stems in large part from the lack of understanding of the diversity and complexity of Puerto Rico and her culture. If Images of Puerto Rico can contribute in some measure to deepening that understanding, it will have fulfilled its overriding purpose.

El Centro, California
July, 1984

Beginnings

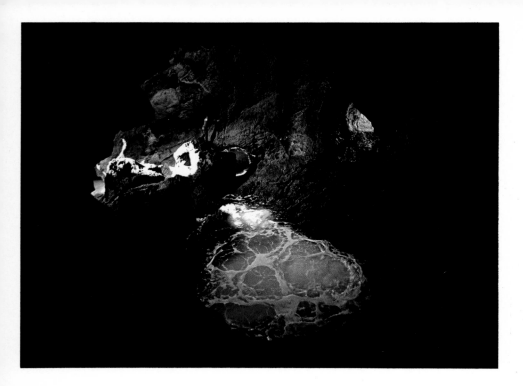

The second culture to occupy the island was the Igneri, or Saladoid, another fishing-hunting society, but one which reached the island from the south, originating in the Saladoid region of the Orinoco Valley of Venezuela and spreading its way up the island chain of the Lesser Antilles. Although the Igneris endured on the island some four hundred years, or until about the sixth century A.D., little is known of their culture, save the fact that they excelled in pottery-making, based on the ceramic artefacts of their period.

Around the time the Igneri culture entered into decline another culture—the Ostionoid—spread northward along the same route from the Orinoco Valley. Like the Igneris, the Ostionoids were a subgroup of the Arawak Indian culture which occupied much of northern South America in this epoch. (One body of archaeological opinion holds that the Ostionoid culture in fact evolved directly out of the Igneri culture in Puerto Rico.) The Ostionoids would, over time, evolve a complex economic and social structure which began to take final form around 1000 A.D., a culture known as the Taíno.

The Ostionoid-Taino society (hereinafter referred to simply as the Taino) differed from the earlier two cultures in many aspects, but one in particular was fundamental: it was based on a developed agriculture, involving the cultivation of a number of native New World plants, including cassava, peanuts, peppers, and cotton. This seemingly simple but enormously consequential difference meant that the Tainos could be—and were—a non-

*A*n October sunrise brings golden hues to the pounding Atlantic at Punta Puerto Nuevo (**preceding page**). It seems a timeless scene—and indeed, the sun has risen over this island astride the border of the Caribbean and the Atlantic for eons. The island's formation began some 150 million years ago, during the Mesozoic Era, the geologists tell us. Its foundation is a volcanic mountain rising from the floor of the sea, and in Puerto Rico's case it is a very high mountain: the Puerto Rico Trench, or Brownson Deep, to the north of the island, has been sounded to over 30,000 feet, making it the deepest known point in the Atlantic Ocean.

And yet even timeless-seeming sunrises can be deceptive: in truth even the scene at Punta Puerto Nuevo is less than 500 years old—for the coconut palms seen silhouetted by the sun, and found all along the island's coastline, did not arrive on the island until the 1500s, brought from the Cape Verde Islands off the African coast. Man has been witnessing sunrises here for far longer than that, however: the most recent archeological evidence indicates that man first made his home on the island some 2000 years ago (and perhaps considerably before that). They were a people of the Archaic culture, who, living by fishing and some hunting and gathering, had spread across the Greater Antilles, probably from Florida. The evidence of their presence on the island has been found primarily in or near several coastal caves (such as the Cueva del Indio near Arecibo, **this page, upper left**, which is decorated with human-like figures carved into the soft limestone, **this page, lower right**). The duration of the Archaic presence in Puerto Rico is not known with certainty, although the fact that they were a non-agricultural, semi-nomadic people suggests that their attachment to any one place was somewhat tenuous.

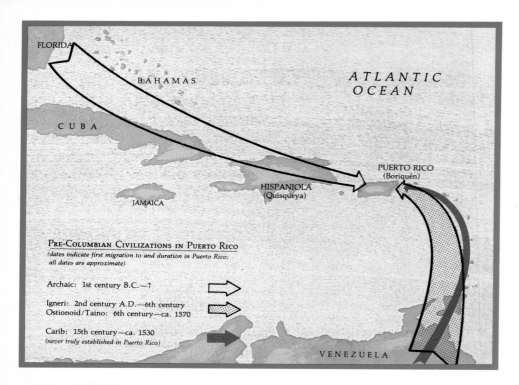

PRE-COLUMBIAN CIVILIZATIONS IN PUERTO RICO
(dates indicate first migration to and duration in Puerto Rico; all dates are approximate)

Archaic: 1st century B.C.—?

Igneri: 2nd century A.D.—6th century
Ostionoid/Taino: 6th century—ca. 1570

Carib: 15th century—ca. 1530
(never truly established in Puerto Rico)

nomadic people, and were able to build permanent villages of bohíos *(thatched huts, like those in the reconstruction of a Taino village at Tibes, near Ponce,* **this page, lower***).* Being able to stay in one locale brought the possibility of developing to a much higher level the physical, social, and ideological aspects of the Taino culture.

Among the survivors of that latter aspect of Taino society is the cemí, a small idol which was fashioned of wood or *(as* **previous page***)* stone, and usually bearing human-like features. The cemíes served as symbols of the Taino deities and were used in both religious rites and in everyday prayer as an aid in communicating with these gods. *(Inhaling a strong tobacco mixture helped reach a mental state conducive to such communication.)*

Perhaps the most elaborate evidence of the Tainos' advanced socio-religious development, however, are the bateyes *(ceremonial ball courts)* where the Tainos performed religious celebrations called areytos, as well as a ball game *(which probably ressembled a rough-and-tumble version of modern-day soccer).* The largest and most developed complex of ball courts found in Puerto Rico—or anywhere, for that matter—is in the Cordillera Central at Caguana, near Utuado. Extensively restored in the early 1950's, the Caguana courts date from about the 12th century, and some *(including the longest, which is seen* **opposite***)* are surrounded by a row of upright stones bearing petroglyphs.

During the course of the 15th century, the Tainos began facing a threat from another culture which had, for some time, been making its way up the Lesser Antilles from Venezuela; it was primarily a nomadic, hunting-based culture, and two of the characteristics of the pre-historic hunting cultures were their aggressivity and their need for a large expanse of territory for survival *(compared to the greater land-efficiency of the agriculturally-based societies such as the Taino).* As a successful culture, with an expanding population, the Caribs, as they called themselves, were continually in need of new territory, and as the century drew to a close the struggle for Boriquén, as the Tainos called the island, was about to begin in earnest.†

That struggle would, indeed, occur—but not with the hunting-based, aggressive Caribs. Rather, the struggle would be with another society altogether, a culture so far removed from the Taino experience that the Taino would not at first even recognize that the newcomers were even mortals, ordinary human beings like themselves. And when they did make this belated recognition, the battle was already lost, for the society of these white men had long before won the battle on the field of technology.

---

† *The name lives on to this day, somewhat modified, as Borinquen, and Puerto Ricans proudly refer to themselves as Borinqueños or Boricuas. Other Taino words have survived (many with modifications) into the modern era as well, such as hammock, canoe, and hurricane, and in the names of island towns such as Caguas, Jayuya, and Utuado.*

(Cemí courtesy Museo de la Universidad de Puerto Rico; actual size about three inches across.)

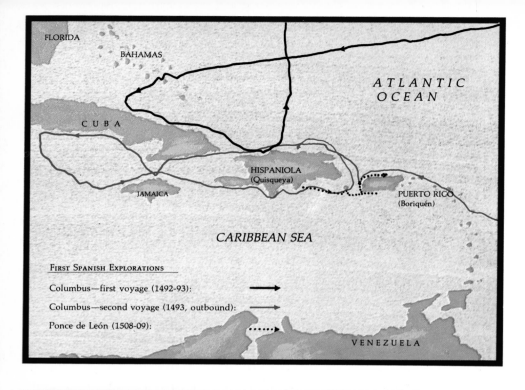

FLORIDA
BAHAMAS

ATLANTIC
OCEAN

CUBA

HISPANIOLA
(Quisqueya)

JAMAICA

PUERTO RICO
(Boriquén)

CARIBBEAN SEA

FIRST SPANISH EXPLORATIONS

Columbus—first voyage (1492-93):

Columbus—second voyage (1493, outbound):

Ponce de León (1508-09):

VENEZUELA

Questing for gold—and for converts to the cross—the conquistadores came, following in the footsteps of those sailors and adventurers who had called their dauntless leader by his Spanish name, Cristóbal Colón (known to English-speakers as Christopher Columbus), and who "Parting from Palos in the Santa María, the Pinta and the Niña, crossed the ocean and saw the dawn of the new world."*

Not until the Great Admiral's second voyage, in 1493 (he would eventually make a total of four voyages to the New World), would he sight and land on the island the Tainos called Boriquén, and which he named San Juan Bautista, after the son of the Spanish kings. (Later, through common usage, the name bestowed upon the principal city, "Puerto Rico"—meaning rich, or exquisite, port—and that given to the island, were, sometime early in the 1500s, exchanged for each other). But Columbus was already sufficiently burdened with the tasks of establishing the colony in nearby Santo Domingo and continuing his explorations to tarry long. His stop was only long enough to reprovision and claim the island for Spain, and after a stay of only two days he hurried on to Hispaniola, leaving sleepy Boriquén and its overawed Taino population to wonder at this incredible development in a theretofore unchanging existence.

Some fifteen years would pass, with the Taino having no further knowledge of these god-like creatures save what they might have learned from any kinsmen from Hispaniola. If they did learn of the Spaniards' activities on neighboring Quisqueya, it could not have been encouraging: for despite some efforts led by Catholic priests to protect them, the Tainos suffered greatly under the Spanish occupation. Needing manual labor to work their gold mines and farms, and, as aspiring gentlemen and people of position, being disinclined to perform such work themselves, the Spanish pressed the Indians into service. Unused to slave labor conditions, and exposed for the first time to European diseases for which they had no immunity, the Taino population was being rapidly decimated. **

In 1508, Juan Ponce de León, who had accompanied Columbus as a soldier on his second, colonizing voyage (in which some 1500 men, and 17 ships, had taken part), and who had later returned to Hispaniola to live, was given the task of colonizing Puerto Rico. He arrived on August 12 of that year with a force of 50 men, landing on the south coast. After exploring the island and discovering the magnificent bay on the north coast, he ordered the colony's first settlement, Caparra, to be established some two miles south of it. Named governor of the colony the following year, Ponce de León would oversee the colony's first, crucial years; but in 1512, lured by the promise of a fountain with miraculous curative powers—a veritable "fountain of youth"—he departed on the voyage which would lead him to the discovery of Florida. (On a second voyage there in 1521 he would be mortally wounded in an Indian skirmish, later to die in Havana. In the mid-16th century his remains were brought back to Puerto Rico to be permanently interred.)

Thus, despite having remained on the island for less than ten years, as the colony's first governor and conquistador, it is to him that history has accorded the glory of being the colony's founder, and his bronze likeness has the place of honor in the plaza next to the Church of San José in Viejo San Juan (**this page, lower right**, and **opposite**, seen in a double exposure).

---

* The quotation (in Spanish) is to be found on a monumental memorial in Madrid's Plaza de Colón, together with the names of all those known to have made what was surely history's most consequential voyage.

** Any fears the Tainos may have formed would prove well-founded: precisely the same pattern would evolve in Puerto Rico, and by the mid-1500s the Indian population as an ethnic group had virtually disappeared, although through extensive intermarriage with the Spanish and African populations the Taino became a permanent part of the island's racial heritage.

page, upper left *an interior view, and* lower right, *the exterior).*

By 1530 the colony still numbered less than 600 white settlers (and some 2000 African slaves), and while the majority continued to reside in or near San Juan, efforts were going forward to settle other areas of the island as well. A town had been established on Guánica Bay as early as 1510, but was soon abandoned; a similar fate befell a settlement at Aguada, on the west coast, the following year. In 1512 a town named San Germán was established, also on the west coast, but its nearness to the sea made it the frequent target of pirate attacks; in 1570 it was moved to a hilly site inland, where it has remained ever since, and thus rightly claims to be the second oldest settlement on the island.

Remarkably, the chapel built on the site in the early 1600s, named Porta Coeli (opposite) *is still in existence (as one of the many museums administered by the Institute of Puerto Rican Culture), the showpiece of San Germán and home to a superb collection of historic carvings of religious figures which once decorated many of the island's churches.*

Other towns or settlements established during the 1500s included Coamo, Arecibo, and Aguada, but by 1590 the European population still numbered only 2500 people. The colony's population growth was, of course, hampered by the hardships such as epidemics and attacks by Indians and pirates, but perhaps the most significant impediment to growth during this period was the arrival of the news of the fabulous wealth discovered by Pizarro in Peru. "May God take me to Peru!" became the cry in the 1530s, and for a time the colony's population actually decreased due to emigration. (So severe was the threat to the colony's very existence that the Spanish authorities declared severe penalties for unauthorized departures.)

*T*he colony would grow slowly in its early years, for, as has been mentioned, the Spanish were occupied in other areas of their new realm, and deposits of gold, eagerly sought and soon found, soon proved to be very limited, and the early Spaniards in the New World were not inclined to remain long where there were not good prospects of finding a fortune in precious metal. But by 1520 a town of some 300 settlers was beginning to take shape on the small island on the northern side of the superb bay (the initial settlement to the south of the bay, at Caparra, had been abandoned after a few years when it became apparent that the open and marshy terrain made the site ideal both for insect propagation and Indian attacks). Although, as has been mentioned, Juan Ponce de León had left in search of fortune and the Fountain of Youth in Florida, his family in 1521 began the construction of a house which would become the finest dwelling in the town; with numerous modifications and renovations it survives to this day (and was, until its recent conversion to a museum, the oldest continuously-inhabited dwelling in the New World), and offers both a superb view of San Juan Bay as well as a glimpse of how a well-to-do family of the colonial gentility lived in the 16th and 17th centuries (this

B ut despite the settlements out on the island, it was San Juan which commanded the primary attention of the Spanish authorities, for the reason which has already been alluded to: with the development of Spain's vastly larger colonies both on the American continents and in the rest of the Caribbean, and with the beginning of regular shipments of gold and silver from those colonies back to the mother country, the need for the protection of those ocean shipments became vital. A glance at a map, and an understanding of the prevailing winds which dictated the route of square-rigged sailing vessels—northeast from Havana, then through the Bahamas Strait and eastward across the Atlantic— will show why: although Puerto Rico is not directly on that route, had it fallen into unfriendly hands the task of protecting those annual treasure convoys would have been greatly complicated. Thus possession of the island was vital, and San Juan and its superb bay were the vital element in maintaining dominance over the island.

So the Spanish crown commenced the construction of the forts and walls which would ensure the city's defense: the very first, begun in 1537, was the palace-fortress which came to be called, simply enough, La Fortaleza—The Fortress. (Casa Blanca, the house of the Ponce de León family dating from 1521, was at times used as a stronghold against Indian attacks, but it had been built primarily as a residence.) Its location was apparently chosen primarily with an eye to ease of access for arriving ships; unfortunately, that location was not the logical choice for the best defense of the harbor, and it soon became apparent that a stronger fort on El Morro (The Headland), dominating the harbor, was indicated. In 1539 construction of that fort, which would be named San Felipe del Morro, was authorized, to be financed from the treasury of the Vice-Royalty of Mexico (New Spain), a subsidy which would continue to be the main financial support of the island's government until the Mexican revolt early in the 19th century. (See "Mi Viejo San Juan" for a further discussion of El Morro).

Repeated pirate attacks at various points on the island during the 16th century, and especially the attacks by Drake in 1595, the Earl of Cumberland in 1598 (the latter succeeding in occupying El Morro for a period of some weeks), and the Dutch in 1625, made it evident that additional fortifications were needed to protect the city and its population from landward attack, and about 1634 construction began on Fort San Cristóbal (**these pages**), at the eastern wall of what was then the city.

San Cristóbal remains today, of course, a magnificent example of European defense construction of the 17th and 18th centuries (and, since 1949, a National Historic Site administered by the National Park Service), and perhaps the island's most visible reminder of the principal role Puerto Rico was to play on the world scene for the more than two centuries following the fort's construction.

(Photograph of San Cristóbal with the assistance of Edgardo Murray Fornes.)

*T*he fact that the Spanish early on came to look at Puerto Rico primarily as a strategic location, of value principally for its role in guarding the sea lanes to other colonies, would be crucial to its development which is to say, the resources and attitude accorded to it by the crown. In the early 17th century Spain was, quite literally, suffering an embarassment of riches—it had discovered and claimed for itself an expanse of territory in the New World many times larger than Spain itself, an expanse so vast that its full extent would not even be fully realized until well into the 19th century. Some of these territories—Peru and Mexico particularly—were proving fabulously rich in gold and silver, while others had vast potential for agricultural development. Spain quite simply had not enough men, money and resources—ships, arms, tools, the whole gamut of materials needed—to successfully establish and maintain all these new colonies.

Faced with this situation, Spain naturally and logically concentrated its resources where the payoff would be greatest. Puerto Rico, lacking in precious metals and tiny alongside the other Spanish colonies, was simply passed by in the rush to richer prizes (even neighboring Hispaniola, not much larger when considered against the immensity of the continents, nonetheless received far more attention and resources, as the first seat of government for Spain's New World possessions.)

There have been many definitions of what constitutes a colony through the years, but one concept is central to the classic definition: a colony exists for the benefit of the mother country. Thus Puerto Rico—too small and poor in metallic wealth to command Spanish attention to developing it, simply languished during most of the 17th and 18th, and even into the 19th centuries. (Some brief histories of the island essentially skip the period from 1625, when the Dutch attacked San Juan, to the American invasion in 1898, with perhaps a brief nod to the unsuccessful English attack of 1797.)†

The island's development was further hampered in this period by Spain's mercantilist trade policies, which restricted colonial commerce to the mother country alone; nonetheless, so stretched were her shipping resources—and so active the pirates in the Caribbean—that periods of years could, and did, pass without a single Spanish commercial vessel calling at the island. In this environment, not surprisingly, smuggling flourished.

The trade monopoly was lifted in 1815, part of a Spanish response to growing agitation in the New World for a "fairer deal," as we might put it today. Philosophies and attitudes toward royal authority were undergoing a sea change throughout the world, and the Americas were at the forefront of this shift. The revolt of the thirteen English colonies, and later, of the Spanish colonies were of course among the most far-reaching expressions of this profound ideological evolution.

In Puerto Rico these winds of change were felt as well, although, given the size of the colony and the make-up of the population (which had acquired many pro-Royalists from other, rebelling, Spanish colonies), they were somewhat muted. Nonetheless, during the course of the 19th century sentiment and agitiation grew for an easing of the harshness of Spanish rule, and the granting of civil and political rights to the colony. The mood for change took two primary courses: the first called for separation—i.e., independence—from Spain; the second, though demanding political and civil liberties identical to those enjoyed in the mother country, sought local self-rule without separation—in a word, autonomy.

The first movement, whose principal leader was a physician named Ramón E. Betances, reached its apogee in 1868 when a band of separatist sympathizers mounted a revolt in Lares, at the northern edge of the coffee country. Quickly suppressed the following day, the revolt had no lasting military consequences, and in fact was the only native challenge of arms ever made against Spanish rule in island history. But during their brief moment of glory the would-be revolutionaries declared the Republic of Puerto Rico, and the gesture became known as El Grito de Lares (The Cry of Lares).

In the ensuing years the Grito de Lares acquired considerable significance as an expression of Puerto Rican identity, and on its anniversary, September 23, the central plaza of the town has become the rallying-point—and the speakers' platform—for those of independentista and nacionalista leanings (**opposite**).

Perhaps the most significant consequence of the Grito de Lares was in the reaction to it: awakened to the possibility of revolt in yet another colony, the Spanish government initiated a policy of extending broader freedoms to the island's inhabitants. The trend was hardly a steady one, however, and the periodic retraction of liberties only aggravated the demand for more equitable treatment, giving impetus to the growing autonomist movement in the latter half of the 19th century.

The autonomist movement had a number of leaders, including Román Baldorioty de Castro and José Celso Barbosa, but the man whose name became synonymous with the autonomy movement, to the point that he is sometimes identified as the "George Washington of Puerto Rico," was Luis Muñoz Rivera, the editor of the liberal newspaper La Democracia. It was he who led the autonomist party's commission to Spain in 1896, and when, the following year, the Spanish government granted the island an Autonomous Charter, it was he who emerged as the undisputed leader of the island's autonomous government. (Today the house in Barranquitas where Muñoz Rivera was born, **this page**, is preserved as a museum.)‡

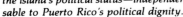

† There were some developments during this period, of course: new towns were settled—by 1750 there were some 14, and by the end of that century another 25, including Ponce, Mayagüez, Fajardo, and Humacao, had been started. The island's population, still only 45,000 in 1765, would triple to over 150,000 in 1800, as the steadily improving agricultural picture continued to attract new immigrants. The early-16th century development of the sugar industry proved short-lived, however, unable to compete with the more advanced technology of the English and French sugar colonies. Cattle (hides), ginger and tobacco would take its place; then in the mid-1700s coffee would be introduced, drawing a sizeable population to the mountainous interior for the first time, and becoming the leading export of the 19th century.

‡ Following the dissolution of the Autonomous Government upon the American invasion, Muñoz Rivera would continue to struggle for local self-rule and civil rights, now under the American flag; he would later serve as the island's Resident Commisioner in Washington, but would die in 1916 without having obtained the plebiscite on the questions of U.S. citizenship and the island's political status—independence, autonomy, or statehood—which he believed indispensable to Puerto Rico's political dignity.

15, 1898, the U.S. battleship Maine *blew up under mysterious circumstances in Havana Harbor, and (with a not-so-gentle nudge from the American press) was to be the justification (or pretext) for the United States to launch into "a splendid little war" with Spain. With Admiral Dewey's destruction of the Spanish fleet at Manila Bay and the swift victory of the U.S. forces in Cuba (where Teddy Roosevelt and his Rough Riders had gained fame in their charge up San Juan Hill), the war was all but over; and when at daybreak on July 25, 1898 the U.S.S. Gloucester steamed into Guánica Bay on the southern coast* (**opposite**), *there remained only seventeen days of hostilities to the Spanish-American War.*

The American force of 16,000 troops, encountering almost no resistance† from the greatly outnumbered and out-gunned Spanish forces, entered Ponce two days later (**this page, lower**), *and began its overland march toward the battle for San Juan.*

That battle, however, would never take place, for on August 13, 1898 Spain and the United States signed the peace agreement ending hostilities, and San Juan was spared the destruction which a fierce assault would have entailed. (The Treaty of Paris, by which Spain formally ceded Puerto Rico to the U.S.,

*B*ut autonomy under the Spanish crown, so long dreamed of, so unexpectedly obtained, which promised so much for the budding sense of Puerto Rican nationhood, would be very short-lived indeed, and once again, as in 1493, Puerto Rico would be at the mercy of developments far beyond its shores.

In 1898 only two Spanish colonies—Cuba and Puerto Rico—remained in the Americas, and both were sufficiently close to be a particularly sharp pain in the side of the United States, whose naval strategists had long recognized the desirability of obtaining a naval base in the Caribbean—and, if possible, of getting the Spanish out. Further, during the 19th century the new American nation had grown strong and vast (and had developed along the way a convenient philosophy of "manifest destiny" to explain the filling in of her "natural boundaries"—indeed, by the end of the century pressures were building to exercise the doctrine beyond the continent, and so bring the "benefits of American civilization to less fortunate peoples").

Whether, under other circumstances, these pressures would have been accomodated will never be known. For on February

was signed on December 10 of that same year.) The city and the island were turned over to the American commander, General John Brooke, who was to be the first American governor of Puerto Rico, on October 18. (The Spanish flag waving over the Arsenal, **this page**, where the last Spanish troops waited several days for a ship to transport them back to Spain, marked it as the last bit of Puerto Rico to remain under Spanish sovereignity. After a recent restoration, the Arsenal, which dates from 1800, today houses offices and galleries of the Institute of Puerto Rican Culture.)

Much has been, and much more will continue to be, written about the Charter of Autonomy granted to Puerto Rico in 1897; opinion varies the whole gamut between the belief that it signalled a new era of self-government for the island, to the opinion that it was merely one more attempt on the part of Spain to forestall growing sentiments for independence. By mid-summer of 1898, when the U.S. troops landed at Guánica Bay, only the first steps toward implementing the terms of the Charter had been taken; the real tests of the interpretation Spain would give the Charter, hence its meaning for Puerto Rican self-government, lay ahead. But in the historical context, perhaps the most important point is this: when the American invasion occurred and thus made the Charter meaningless, the potential for self-government under the Charter was an unknown—and certainly the men who had struggled to achieve it had the highest expectations for it.

Therefore when the Americans, uncertain of what to do with their new possession, and unaccustomed to the rule of colonial power, installed first a military government, and then a civilian government which provided for even less local autonomy than had been promised under the Autonomic Charter, the disillusionment of those leaders was inevitable. It was a disillusionment which would color the whole history of American involvement with Puerto Rico, and, indeed, which has ramifications into the present day.

---

† Indeed, the Puerto Rican populace, aware of the level of prosperity and civil liberties existing in the States, and hopeful that the American invasion meant a similar future for the island (whether as a part of the United States or as an independent nation) in general welcomed the U.S. troops.

Heritage

The central plaza and Church of San Antonio de Padua in Guayama
(dating from 1736).

The Church of San Miguel in Utuado (dating from 1872).

Church was the official religion of the state, and, as has been mentioned, the conquistadores—at least in theory—conquered the New World as much for God as for gold; but to say only this leaves much unsaid about the role the church would play in a small, distant, poor and "uncivilized" colony such as Puerto Rico.

Even had Puerto Rico been a more important colony than it was to the Spanish crown, and even had Spain's government had the resources to provide a significant governmental presence throughout the island, the fact is that the concept of governmental responsibility for public welfare was vastly different from that held today in the developed world. Furthermore, during Puerto Rico's first centuries as a Spanish colony the men of the church were often the principal—if not the only—educated members of the community; even beyond that time, the people's spiritual commitment to the church meant that the church was often able to command resources, both human and material, in excess of those available to the government. (The relative importance of the Church in the life of the people during this epoch is graphically illustrated in virtually every town on the island by both the location of its Catholic church—either in or facing on the central plaza—and by the fact that the church is

*T*he American invasion may have resulted in the departure of the Spanish troops and the striking of the Spanish flag, but it could hardly extinguish four centuries of Spanish culture. Besides the Spanish language and family and social relationships, perhaps the most important element of that culture was the Catholic Church (symbolized **opposite** by a crucifix standing in the stillness of Ponce's Nuestra Señora de Guadalupe Cathedral). It is difficult for most Americans, attuned to a world of extensive governmental activity in nearly all spheres of modern life, and imbued with the concept of the separation of church and state activities, to comprehend the pervasive role played by the Church during the early centuries of Spanish America. Throughout Spain's tenure in Puerto Rico the Catholic

almost invariably the most imposing of the town's older buildings. Two of the most striking examples of these physical reminders of the Spanish era are the churches in Guayama and Utuado (**see previous pages**). The result was that the church functioned not merely as a spiritual institution, but a social institution in the widest sense: dispenser of knowledge and charity, arbiter of disputes, catalyst for community action, and perhaps not least of all, provider of activities which, while fundamentally religious in nature, also contain elements of what today we think of as entertainment.

The role of the Catholic Church in Puerto Rico today is in no way as all-encompassing as it once was (indeed, that role has been diminishing for some time: as early as 1898 a

military chaplain with the invading American forces had remarked that "Puerto Rico is a Catholic country without a religion"), and during this century, the protestant religions, and especially the proselytizing churches, have made strong gains. But, despite these developments, and despite the loss of its position as the official state religion since the American takeover of the island, the Catholic Church remains the majority religion of the country and continues to be a vital element in the lives of a great number of Puerto Ricans, as illustrated in these scenes photographed in Hormigueros, where a woman performs a penitence (**previous pages, top left**) by climbing the steps to the Church of Our Lady of Monserrate on her knees, and a multitude of the faithful take part in an annual feast day procession (**previous pages, lower right**).

While the religious fervor and devotion which inspire scenes such as those photographed in Hormigueros (**previous pages**) remain a vital part of life for many Puerto Ricans, and while the majority of the

or offering the chance to wager at picas (mechanical horse races and other games of chance), dances, musical groups, and, de rigueur, the naming of one or more queens of the town for the coming year. In Ponce (**this page, upper left**) the celebrations are, as is traditional, held in and around the town plaza, and are especially elaborate, including a climax of floats and marchers parading through the streets; since the day of the patroness (Our Lady of Guadalupe) falls in mid-December, the parade celebrates the coming of Christmas as well, complete with Santa Claus.

Yet another of Ponce's major festivities with a religious origin is Carnival, the pre-Lenten revelry traditional in many Catholic societies. Ponce's Carnival is most characterized by its vejigantes (**this page, lower right**), masked and costumed "devils" whose role it is to chase and frighten small children, who in turn egg them on with rhyming taunts. Their name derives from their traditional weapon, an inflated vejiga (the bladder of a pig or young calf), with which they bash any slow-moving or unwary taunters.

country continues to be baptized in and state their adherence to the Catholic church, few would argue that such scenes today typify the average Puerto Rican's approach to his faith. Rather, that devotion today is more likely to be internalized; and, at the same time, as in much of the rest of the world, many public festivities which owe their origins to religious celebrations have become increasingly secular in nature.

Nowhere is this more apparent than in the fiestas patronales, the annual week-long festivals held in virtually every town on the island around the date of the town's patron saint day. No more than a few decades ago these celebrations were nearly exclusively religious in origin, and of course the religious element remains, in the form of special masses and often a procession through the streets of the town bearing an image of the saint (in the case of coastal communities the statue will often be transferred to a boat and part of the procession will be on water). But today the emphasis, at least in terms of public participation, is on the non-religious, and will invariably include (**see these pages**) carnival rides, booths hawking all varieties of food and drink,

*T*he tradition of the Ponce Carnival vejigante masks supports a small group of artisans (like Miguel Angel Caraballo, shown **this page** in his dining room-workshop in Playa de Ponce, and the renowned Juan Alindato, also of Playa de Ponce) who produce the papier-mache masks not only for Carnival but, increasingly, with the upswelling of interest in traditional Puerto Rican culture, for use as decoration in both private homes and in commercial buildings. (An indication of the growing interest in this aspect of traditional artisanry was the recent publication of a book—with a concurrent museum exhibition—on the subject of Ponce's Carnival masks by one of the leading investigators of Puerto Rico's popular culture, Teodoro Vidal of San Juan).

Perhaps the most famous of the fiestas patronales however, are those held during July in Loíza, and honoring St. James the Apostle. (Loíza, a seacoast town a few miles to the east of San Juan, whose population consists largely of the descendants of black slaves, is one of a handful of towns which have come to celebrate a saint other than their town's actual patron. As is not uncommon, in Loíza's case the origin of this practice involves an allegedly miraculous appearance of an image of St. James.)

St. James has a prominent place in Spanish culture owing to the legend of his miraculous assistance to the Spanish Christians in driving the Moors from Iberia, and the Loíza festivities, probably the most colorful and heavily-attended of all the island's patron saint festivals, involve a characterization of that historic event: on the one side the Spanish caballeros, or knights (as the one, **opposite page**, staring out of his wire-mesh mask), and on the other, the vejigantes, representing the Moors, or devils, in this blending of history and allegory (the latter masks, of hollowed-out coconuts, are unique to Loíza).

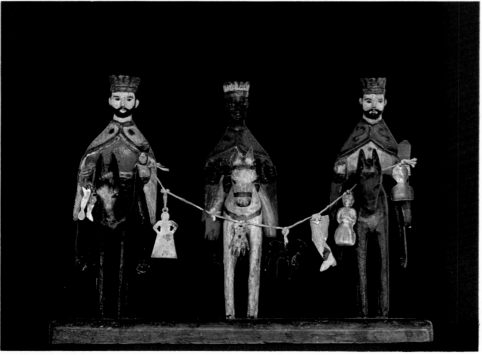

One of the most charming contributions of religion to Puerto Rico's popular culture has been the creation of a folk art or imagery usually referred to simply as santos (saints). Ordinarily measuring a foot or less in height, carved of native woods and then usually painted, the santos are representations of various saints and other religious figures of importance in the Puerto Rican culture. Although today far less common, except as collector's pieces, at one time virtually every Puerto Rican household, especially in the countryside, would contain at least one of these figurines, to which prayers would be directed. The custom owes its origin in part to the fact that Catholic churches typically contained one or more large statues of saints or other holy figures (such as those gathered in the Porta Coeli museum, seen in "Beginnings"), and to the difficulty of going to church services posed by rural living when roads were few and difficult to travel. A santo in the household—perhaps blessed by the parish priest—would provide a comforting reminder of God's presence, even in the isolation of the countryside.

Extant Puerto Rican santos date from the early days of the Spanish settlement of the island, although the great bulk were probably carved between the mid-19th to mid-20th centuries. Many were produced by craftsmen who lived in the Cordillera Central, although many examples abound from the northern coastal plain as well. (It seems appropriate to call these men craftsmen, rather than artists, because that is doubtless how they considered themselves: virtually none of the older santos is signed or dated, making their ascription to a particular craftsman or era a matter for experts, and even then often a matter of conjecture.) The men who carved these figurines over the centuries, known as santeros, were probably men much like Carlos Vázquez of Barrio Cordillera, just outside Ciales, (**opposite**), who still carves today in his workshop behind his home. Part-time carpenter, farmer, and in his earlier years, general laborer, Mr. Vázquez may spend weeks on a single piece; he was working on special order for an unpainted set of the Three Kings on the day I visited. "Sure, I'd like to work as a santero full time," he commented, "but there just isn't the demand . . . . The time when people look on these santos as religious figures is past; today I carve mainly for collectors—not many tourists appreciate the quality involved in my type of hand carving."

On **this page** are two splendid examples of the santero craft: **upper**, a detail of "San Telmo," a modern carving by Tomás Collazo, overall height about eleven inches (courtesy Dr. Ricardo Alegría); and **lower**, the "Three Kings" by the Cabán group of Camuy, late 19th century, about nine inches in height (courtesy Teodoro Vidal).

*W*hile the santeros *are indisputably the most venerated craftsmen of the Cordillera Central, Puerto Rico has had the good fortune to have retained a good many artisans in many fields, scattered throughout the island, who are keeping alive many of the island's traditional handicrafts and artisanry. In my months on the island I met several of these artisans, two of whom are depicted here:*

In the past century, and in the early years of this one, Moca, near the northwestern corner of the island, was, together with nearby Aguadilla and Isabela, the center for the production of bobbin lace, in Puerto Rico called mundillo *(after the word for the revolving frame on which it is made,* **this page, upper**). *During its heyday, thousands of women worked in this cottage industry, earning extra money for the household; but with the island's rising prosperity in this century, and the constantly increasing competition of foreign machine-made lace, the industry and the tradition all but disappeared.*

Only a handful of traditional mundillo *artisans remain: one of the most renowned is Doña María Lasalle of Moca (***this page, lower***), who has been making lace for sixty-three of her seventy years. "I began making lace when I was seven years old—not very well, of course!" she said with a laugh. "School? No, there were no schools for it then—I learned like all the girls did, by watching the older girls and women." (Today, with the sharp reduction in practitioners of the craft, and a surging demand for learning it, a division of the University of Puerto Rico offers classes in* mundillo, *as well as in other traditional handicrafts.)*

*Several months later, once again in the Cordillera Central, in an area known as El Jobo (near Orocovis), I would meet Julio Negrón Rivera (***opposite***), one of the island's master craftsmen of the* cuatro, *a lilting instrument of ten strings unique to Puerto Rico. (In answer to the obvious question, why "cuatro" for an instrument of ten strings?—the answer is that the modern instrument evolved from an original four strings, to which a fifth was later added, and then all five were doubled.) I had arrived early, and after shooting some photographs of him at his workbench, he insisted I stay for some breakfast; while we ate, a morning shower began, and I had the chance to hear an accomplished* cuatro *player accompany himself in singing a song of his own composition, on a masterwork created with his own hands. It was a moving experience, and I thanked Don Julio for posing, for breakfast, and for the entertainment.*

Jíbaro

*T*here is a monument, high in the Cordillera Central, next to the high-speed autopista *traversing the island, just where it begins its plunge toward the arid southern littoral. It features a white stone grouping of a mother, a father, and an infant. It is a monument to the Puerto Rican* jíbaro, *and on it, in Spanish, is inscribed:*

The *jíbaro* is the man of our land, the cultivator of our soil, the genesis of our people, and the authentic expression of Puerto Rico

The *jíbaro* has always been the symbol of our collective identity and the synthesis of the virtues of the people of Puerto Rico

To the Puerto Rican *jíbaro* homage from a grateful people

It has been suggested that there is a certain irony to this monument, notwithstanding the sincerity of the sentiment expressed, due to the fact that "while everyone romanticizes the jíbaro, *nobody wanted to remain one." There is an element of truth in the suggestion, stemming from the fact that the life of the* jíbaro, *at least until the very recent past, was one of nearly unrelenting hardship. But those who see only the irony in this monument are perhaps missing the real point: every society forms a collective ideal of itself, and in honoring the* jíbaro, *Puerto Rico has chosen to identify itself with the* jíbaro *traits of self-reliance, independence, and love of the soil, family, and life itself.*

There is an irony, too, from the perspective of the outsider just getting to know Puerto Rico and accustomed to thinking of her as a tropical island, in realizing that Puerto Ricans see themselves as a people of the mountains. The reasons why Puerto Ricans have come to identify themselves with the mountains of the Cor-

dillera Central are both simple and complex: at the simplest level, the climate in the Cordillera is generally much more agreeable (and in times past, more healthful) than the hot, humid coastal plain, and, even in this day of air conditioning, the change in your spirits as you drive into the cool, often misty reaches of the Cordillera can be remarkable. In times past the mountains also offered safety from raiding Indians, pirates, and the reach of Spanish authorities.

But few people have the luxury of choosing where to live based on these factors alone; today, and even more so in the past, economic considerations predominate. And in the case of Puerto Rico, it was the coming of coffee to the island in the mid-1700s which transformed the rugged Cordillera, drawing in people to grow and work the crop which would become in time the economic mainstay of the colony, of the Cordillera, and of its mountain people, the jíbaro. The close of the 19th century would bring an end to coffee's position as the island's leading export crop, but to this day it dominates the economic life of towns like Adjuntas, Utuado, Maricao, and a dozen others in the moist western central part of the Cordillera.

Even for this crop so intimately entwined with the life of the Cordillera, however, changes are coming: near Adjuntas I visited with José Navarro, foreman of a medium-sized coffee finca in the Guilarte region (shown, **this page, lower** at the wheel of his jeep talking with some pickers). Mr. Navarro's principal problem these days is labor: "You just can't get pickers to do this work, like you could before. It's the cupones," he complained, referring to food stamp payments. "That's why we mostly pick coffee al raspe now (**this page, upper**, a picker at work), pulling the green-ripe beans along with the red-ripe maduro (**opposite**). The quality's not the same, but it goes much faster." Later he would show me an area of the farm where the coffee shrubs were planted in neat rows, open to the sun. "This is the future," he said. "No shade trees—three to four times the production, and lower labor costs. In some places we have nylon mesh on the ground to catch the beans that fall—then we just scoop them up."

*I*ncreased productivity is vital to the coffee industry, already subsidized by the government, if it is to avoid the fate which has befallen another crop, tobacco, which was once second only to coffee in importance in the Cordillera. Native to the West Indies, Columbus found the Tainos using tobacco for pleasure and religious ceremonies, and carried it back to Europe. Its use quickly spread and became a virtual necessity, but monopolistic Spanish trade policies meant a limited market for Puerto Rican tobacco; with access to the American market and capital in this century, production boomed in the drier eastern regions of the Cordillera (seen **this page**, looking east from a point near Ciales). Comerío (**following spread, right-hand page**), at the center of this region, became the "capital" of the tobacco growing area, where earlier in this century thousands of people found employment in the growing, harvesting, curing and production processes. That day is now gone, victim of cheaper foreign production and the high productivity of large-scale U.S. domestic producers.

A handful of small-scale producers like José Alicea (**opposite**) remain, with their production principally destined for use as cigar filler. During the course of the century Puerto Rico has gone from being a significant exporter of tobacco to being a large-scale importer, principally for cigarettes. (Some weeks earlier I had visited a tiny cigar factory in Old San Juan, where the owner commented:"It's a shame—Puerto Rico was once a big cigar producer. Now there's just me and one or two other small fábricas. There's no future in cigars in Puerto Rico. Even the leaf I use here is imported from Honduras; the supply here is too undependable, and besides, it doesn't make good wrapper leaves.")

ty of paved roads in Latin America (the scene **this page, upper left** was photographed on the highway linking Utuado and Arecibo, near Dos Bocas Lake). Only after driving the curves and switchbacks of these roads for several weeks did I come to realize the enormity of that achievement, for the ruggedness and seasonal downpours of the Cordillera presented an enormous obstacle to the roadbuilders. Even today the roads are so often blocked by fallen trees after a heavy downpour that many residents of the mountain areas carry an ax handy in their vehicles.

Good all-weather highways meant that for the first time it was feasible for farm owners and laborers to live some distance from their mountain fincas, and many opted to live in the mountain towns, deserting the lifestyle built around the traditional haciendas. A few of these old plantation houses have been converted to country inns, called paradores, but many others today stand abandoned, or in the care of a trusted employee (like this old coffee plantation house, **this page, lower right**, in the mountains above Yauco), reminders of a bygone era.

*T*here is a sense of constancy to the Cordillera Central, of time moving slowly, and its towns nestled in the valleys have an idyllic air. But this image of changelessness is a deceptive one, for in fact during the past forty years a massive migration from the Cordillera's hillsides and valleys has occurred, into towns like Comerío (**opposite**), which have burst their old boundaries with the arrival of the newcomers. It is the classic rural-urban migration which has been taking place the world over. In Puerto Rico's case it was facilitated by the construction of an extensive network of highways in the Cordillera, principally between 1900 and 1950, which have given the island the highest densi-

*T*he two scenes shown on these pages illustrate two of the most time-honored pastimes of life for the jíbaro, and throughout the Puerto Rican countryside. The traditional pleasures were necessarily simple ones, and despite the competing attractions of today's greater prosperity, they have remained central to the experience of rural life not only in the Cordillera but on the island as a whole.

The "Sport of Gentlemen" it is called in the countryside, and the tradition of the gallera (**this page**), where fighting cocks are brought together to do battle, is one of the oldest in the Spanish world, and probably arrived with the first colonists. (Indeed, cockfighting has an ancient history, dating back to the Persian Empire, Classical Greece, and even before, making it one of the world's oldest pastimes.) The cockfights, usually held on Sunday and one other day during the week, are of course as much a social occasion, and a chance to test one's wagering skill, as much as a sport. The name derives from the fact that bets are placed (and honored) solely on the palabra de caballero, *the word of a gentleman, without any written confirmation.*

The scene **opposite**, although photographed in the town of Hatillo on the north coast, is so typical that it could have been photographed in front of any colmado anywhere on the island. Though the setting may vary, it shows what is probably the oldest and most honored pastime of all: good friends gathering over a drink and talking into the night, about anything under the sun.

While thousands of jíbaros left their hillside homes for the mountain towns, still more deserted the Cordillera altogether, settling in and around San Juan and other coastal cities, where jobs or a better education beckoned. And with the advent of cheap long distance flights after World War II, still more thousands left for the chance at a better life in the States. (An estimated 600,000 Puerto Ricans left the island for the mainland during the '50s and '60s; in the '70s a considerable—but much smaller—number returned to the island to live, usually in the San Juan metropolitan area.) This veritable human flood out of the Cordillera during the past four decades has given rise to the notion that the jíbaro has vanished from the Puerto Rican scene, lured away by the promise of a better and easier life elsewhere. But it is a mistaken conclusion: true, the grim conditions once an inevitable part of life in the Cordillera are much alleviated, but the essential traits of the jíbaro ideal—honesty, self-reliance, hospitality, and attachment to the soil—remain very much the

characteristics of the people of the Cordillera.

In the coffee-rich mountains above Adjuntas I met a family perhaps not untypical of modern jíbaro life. Domingo and Emilia Rivera are both well along in years, he ailing with a heart condition and arthritis in his hands; their simple but sturdy wooden house (**these pages**), painted a bright blue and topped with a corrugated metal roof, sits just a few yards off the road to Mount Guilarte. They raise coffee on their 15 cuerdas, their one cash crop; Mr. Rivera's pension check from earlier years working on a government road crew supplements their income, as does an occasional money order from their five grown children who live in the States; most of their food comes from their own land. A young grandson lives with them; their youngest son works at the nearby government coffee experimental station.

I met the Riveras by simply stopping at their house one day and explaining what I was doing in Puerto Rico; their response was open-armed hospitality, insisting that I see the finca, stay for lunch, and return again soon so that I could see coffee being picked. I did return, three more times, coming away with one of my fondest images of Puerto Rico, and very much reassured that the jíbaro of the Cordillera Central is alive and well. They posed for me in their house (**this page**), holding photographs of some of their children who live in the States, and who have rarely or never returned to the island; indeed, this is one of the great sadnesses for many of Puerto Rico's jíbaros—the loss of their children gone to seek a better life.

The photograph on the wall above the Riveras had an interesting history: they told me that years ago, when just newlyweds, they were returning home from a day of work in the campo when a travelling photographer selling his services came along. They agreed to have their picture taken, asking a moment to change out of their work clothes. "Oh, don't worry about that," they were told, and the photographer snapped the picture then and there. Some weeks later he brought the retouched portrait back, showing the couple in their Sunday best!

One thing that did characterize the jíbaro households I got to know was that they were generally people well along in years, whose children had opted for a life outside the Cordillera; if this trend continues unabated, then a sight I came to view with great fondness—the snug jíbaro house tucked neatly into the mountain stillness (**opposite**)—may one day truly vanish from the Puerto Rican scene altogether.

Island

W hile the ideal of the jíbaro and his life in the Cordillera Central remain at the heart of Puerto Rico's
self-image, it is nonetheless on the surrounding
coastal plain where the great majority of the island's people today live and work.† It has in fact long been so, and even during
the heyday of coffee and tobacco production in the 19th century the Cordillera probably held a smaller population than the
lowlands.

The turn of this century brought new economic vitality to
the coastal areas, and the causal element was the American invasion of 1898 which brought a new colonial master to Puerto
Rico. The island's coffee producers had grown prosperous during the course of the 19th century in part because their sales in
the Spanish market were assured a high price, thanks to Spain's
tariff on foreign-grown beans. After 1898, no longer Spanish
territory, Puerto Rico lost that preferential market. The United
States, on the other hand, lacking the climatic conditions for
domestic production, had no tariff protection for coffee producers, and the island suddenly found itself forced to compete
against the States' traditional suppliers such as Brazil and
Colombia, veritable coffee giants. And by a cruel coincidence,
at the turn of the century the island's coffee growers were particularly ill-suited to enter the competitive fray: in 1899 Hurricane San Ciriaco, to this day the worst hurricane to strike
Puerto Rico since the arrival of the Spanish (in Puerto Rico,
hurricanes were traditionally named for the saint day on which
they occurred), swept through the Cordillera, devastating the
coffee shrubs, and worse, their vital shade tree cover.

Though the coffee growers would eventually get their fincas
back into production, coffee would never regain its dominant
place in the Puerto Rican economy. For the same U.S. tariff
structure which denied protection to coffee would prove a
boon to another historic island crop. In 1898 the island's era of
"King Sugar" was about to begin (**this page**, an aerial view of
the cane fields east of Ponce).

---

† Indeed, the fact that most Puerto Ricans have long been removed from
the reality of jíbaro life probably has contributed to the creation of that
ideal—just as America's identification with the cowboy has intensified
apace with its becoming a nation of city-dwellers.

Sugar was hardly new to the island: in fact, beginning in the 1530s and continuing for a century afterwards, sugar had been the island's most important crop; but a combination of factors—including competition from other, more productive Caribbean islands, the lack of native capital to invest in the latest technologies, and Spain's restrictive trade policies and indifference to development of the island's economic potential—brought the industry's decline in the mid-1600s.‡ The coming of the American flag and troops would change the picture dramatically: now sugar produced on the island would have free access to the American market, and American capital could now be invested without fear of foreign expropriation.

*I*t had long been recognized that the southern coastal plain, blessed with the best soils on the island, had all the requirements for the successful growing of sugar cane, except one: the average annual rainfall on much of the plain was far below the minimum—about 75 inches per year—required for cane. The potential for damming and channeling the excess water in the rivers which ran (mainly to the north) out of the Cordillera Central had also been recognized; but without the economic factors which would guarantee the success of a sugar industry, such thoughts were merely extravagant dreams.

Thus after 1898 Puerto Rico presented a ripe opportunity for large American corporate sugar interests: within a few years they had bought up most of the arable acreage along the northern coastal plain, planted cane and built sugar mills. And by 1910 they had persuaded the island's compliant legislature to

‡ Though sugar production declined, it never disappeared entirely, and during the great agricultural surge of the 19th century became once again an important export crop. Nonetheless the early decline of the sugar industry in Puerto Rico helps explain why slavery never developed on the island to the extent that it did on many of the other (especially English and French) islands of the Caribbean, for the primary demand for slave labor in the West Indies came from the growth and prosperity of the sugar plantation system. After the initial few decades of the colony's history (when they considerably outnumbered the white population), African slaves in Puerto Rico apparently never constituted more than about 12 per cent of the population, in contrast to some of the English islands in the Caribbean, for example, where the figure exceeded 80 per cent.

commence the building of dams and the attendant irrigation networks which would bring water to the arid coastal areas south of the Cordillera. This vast corporate expansion of the island's sugar industry would have some lasting side benefits as well: the irrigation system (such as the one shown **opposite page, upper** on the Aguirre plantation) entailed the construction of dams, which generated electricity in addition to supplying water to the canals, and the surplus power was sold, thus bringing electricity to many areas for the first time; the necessity of transporting the cane from the fields to the centrales (sugar mills) also led to the construction of a railroad network from the cane fields to the mills, which was eventually extended to provide general freight and passenger service around and across the island as well. That latter aspect of train service disappeared about 1950, falling victim to the motor vehicle and the highways which had been constructed since the turn of the century. Though limited rail networks continue to haul cane from the fields to the mills, the only passenger service available now is a nostalgic tourist ride near Arroyo using an old locomotive which once served Central Lafayette (**opposite page, lower**).

The island's sugar industry, which in 1897 had exported less than 65,000 tons of sugar, would in 1910 produce some 350,000 tons; and ten years after that, nearly half a million. The figures would continue rising steadily to over a million tons in 1938, then would level off during the war years, to reach a new peak of more than 1,300,000 tons in 1952.† But from that point on, and arguably even earlier, the island's sugar industry was in trouble. The hand cutting which had historically been such a familiar scene in the cane growing areas (**this page, upper**) has now largely disappeared, as the industry has shifted to mechanization (**this page, lower**, a mechanical harvester on the Aguirre Plantation) to reduce labor costs, but nonetheless the island's production costs have remained substantially above those of competing countries, and on a per-pound basis, well above the world market price, thus ensuring an operating loss.

† Meanwhile in the Cordillera, the coffee production levels of the late 19th century—which themselves were far below the levels attained in the mid-1800s—would not be reached again until 1910-20, then would decline precipitously.

To see the modern sugar industry firsthand I visited the Aguirre mill and plantation on Jobos Bay, the largest of four mills still refining cane into sugar on the island in 1984—Central Roig near Yabucoa was producing only molasses, the raw material for rum production. (As recently as the early 1970s there were 25 mills still operating.) The scenes (**this page** and **opposite**), of the cane dump and of some mill workers cleaning the fire chamber of one of the boilers were shot there during the 1984 crop season.)

Outwardly, the mill seemed to be operating normally—but after a time, it became apparent that initial appearances were deceptive: one of the two grinding lines had been shut down indefinitely, with no plans to restart it, and the rail cars coming in from the cane fields were arriving only two-thirds full. In fact, the mill was operating at less than half of capacity, and even to run at this level cane was being trucked in at great cost from distant fields.

With a stagnant or declining world sugar price over the past few decades, and increasing production from lower-cost sugar producing countries, Puerto Rico's sugar industry has become caught in a descending spiral of rising labor costs, decreased acreage, closing mills, and insufficient production to adequately supply even the handful of mills that remain; the result is a very inefficient operation being kept alive only with huge government subsidies. Present production costs are rumored to be over twice the world sugar price, and, in perhaps the ultimate irony, the island now imports most of its requirements of refined (white) sugar, since the island's one refinery is too small to meet local demand. (It should perhaps be pointed out that the ordinary sugar central processes cane only to the semi-refined 'raw sugar' stage).

Thus the fact is that Puerto Rico's sugar industry today hangs by a thread—that thread being the government's willingness to continue subsidizing the several thousand jobs still provided by the industry, at a cost that was running into the tens of millions of dollars annually in the mid-1980s.

*H*ow much longer the island's sugar industry will survive is of course of paramount concern to the remaining industry workers like boiler-cleaner Marcelo Meléndez (**this page**), whom I photographed at the Aguirre mill. Like most of his fellow mill workers, he is well along in years, and just hopes the mill will continue running until he reaches retirement age. Not that the work is easy: as another of the boiler-cleaners remarked, wiping the sweat from his brow, "If you can take the heat from this job, you can do any job at all." The problem, of course, is that in the present Puerto Rican economy finding another job— much less a job that pays as well as do jobs in the mills—will be a difficult task.

While jobs in the sugar industry have always been sought after, wages and working conditions were not always as enviable as they are today; indeed, it is commonly agreed that life for the cane workers during the first half of the century (not to mention the earlier era) was an arduous one indeed. Perhaps the most eloquent depiction of that life is a play entitled Tiempo Muerto, by Puerto Rico's most renowned living dramatist, Manuel Méndez Ballester (seen **opposite** on the play's set during a 1984 revival in Old San Juan's Tapia Theatre).

The play's title is a double entendre, and suggests its underlying theme: "tiempo muerto" in the cane industry refers to the off, or "dead" season, when there is no work for the harvest crews; but the literal translation of the term is "dead time," or perhaps, "time killed"—and the play speaks of the tragedy of wasted lives and the sense of entrapment inherent in the economic and social order that was generated by the plantation system.

Performed for the first time in 1940 (Mr. Méndez had worked as a youth in Central Coloso on the island's west coast before beginning a varied career as author, journalist, theatrical producer and legislator), the play has become one of the most famous and enduring works in Puerto Rican drama.

*T*he great expansion of the cane industry early in this century altered not only the landscape; it changed styles of living as well. Along the southern coastal plain especially, where previously the sparse rainfall had supported only a scattered population, the societal and cultural impact of the new industry was enormous: entire company towns grew up around the largest centrales, like Aguirre and Guánica. But after the peak production years of the 1950s the American companies, faced with a bleak prospect for the industry in Puerto Rico brought on by escalating wages, repeated labor strife, and above all, by the competition from lower-cost areas, began a retrenching, closing down mills (the rusting remains of a score of mills are dotted around the island), reducing planted acreage, and eventually selling out their interests to the island's government.

The towns around the mills have taken on a faded look, although some are still populated (at this writing, the only mill on the southern coast still operating is Aguirre). But there remain enough houses and buildings in good condition (like the manager's house at the Aguirre mill, **this page**, and the little woodframe church at the Central Guánica, **opposite**) to evoke a feeling of what life in the company towns must have once been.

the expansion of the dairy industry has probably now reached its natural limits. (The dairy industry, which in terms of dollar value is now the most important sector of the agricultural economy, currently supplies all the island's fresh milk requirements.)

With the island currently importing the bulk of its food consumption, and a great deal of land lying fallow or underutilized, the potential for the expansion of fruit and vegetable production seems enormous. Already a considerable proportion of the island's requirements of fresh fruit and staples such as bananas, oranges, and plantains are produced domestically, mainly on the slopes of the Cordillera Central, but the greatest potential for food production would seem to be on the southern plain where cane land is steadily being taken out of production.

A number of innovative farmers are leading the way with such modern techniques as drip and sprinkler irrigation, plastic ground cover for weed control, and

*T*he decline in the island's sugar fortunes has had a number of consequences outside the immediate industry: although one mill now produces molasses alone, less than a quarter of the country's molasses requirements for its rum industry (the world's largest) can be met from island sources, and the rum producers have increasingly had to turn to foreign sources for their supply of cane molasses, the raw material from which all rum is distilled (pictured, **this page, upper left** is one of the aging rooms at the Serrallés distillery near Ponce).

And as sugar cane acreage has declined, the one-time cane land all over the island has largely been converted to pasture for beef and dairy herds (**this page, lower right**, a herd of Holsteins grazes in the early morning light near Barceloneta on the north coast). But despite one of the highest per-capita milk consumption rates in the world—fueled by the relative youth of the population and the copious consumption of café con leche—

carefully monitored fertilization. One of the largest such ventures is an Israeli-owned farm growing a variety of crops, including melons, tomatos and pimientos on former cane land near Salinas. On another, owned by a Puerto Rican company near Guánica, similar techniques are being applied to 800 acres of eggplant, pimientos, tomatos and melons. (As an indication of the excitement these efforts are creating on the island—where people have come to take for granted the idea that Puerto Rico can no longer produce its own food—a television film crew, **this page, lower left**, was interviewing the manager for an evening newscast on the day I visited the farm near Guánica.

Despite oft-heard allegations that Puerto Ricans are no longer willing to do farm labor, the farms I saw seem to have no difficulty in recruiting enough workers at the federal minimum wage. Indeed, for workers like Eddie Muñiz (**this page, upper right**), who have seen jobs in the area evaporate with the recent closing of the Central

Guánica, the wage is just fine: "And it's steady work—I can work here all year around, not like in the cane, where the harvest started in January and lasted maybe only six months."

The projects I saw are a promising start—perhaps most valuable for demonstrating what can be done, given the will and the confidence to make the attempt—but obviously they will have to be multiplied manyfold if they are to make any meaningful dent in a food import bill close to the $2 billion mark.

over 50 years—one of many built in a similar style throughout the island in that era.) And it bears stressing that this infrastructure was built almost entirely from island-generated resources—although the 1930s brought an infusion of New Deal projects, it was not until the 1960s that federal funds would begin to play a significant role in the island's finances.

Of equal importance, the economic activity generated by the industry resulted in the first significant growth of a middle class of merchants, managers and professionals in the towns which prospered in the cane-growing areas. It is in the towns in the south—favored by a dry climate and to an extent bypassed by the explosion of building which has occurred in the past two decades—where many of the most charming houses built in this era are best preserved. Particularly striking are some of the houses of Guayama, Yauco, Guánica, and Mayagüez (on the west coast), and San Germán (**this page, upper left**), where this gem is to be found opposite the Porta Coeli chapel.

*I*n the recent past it has become fashionable to stress the "exploitation" aspects of the sugar industry during the period of its ownership by large American-based corporations, sometimes losing sight of the fact that concepts of appropriate wage levels and working conditions have changed enormously the world over in the past half-century. Despite the problems and conditions the plantation system produced, and despite the remittance of large profits to absentee owners, it is an indisputable fact that the era of King Sugar generated an economic base which permitted the island to make tremendous strides in building its physical infrastructure of schools, roads, bridges, railroads, and water and electrical systems (graphic reminders of that era are the concrete bridges spanning the rivers and streams of the Cordillera Central—the dedication stones tell the story: "Built 1927, Horace M. Towner, Governor . . . ." Another, in the town of Salinas, is the still-handsome public market, **opposite**, in continuous use for

*B*ut it is unquestionably Ponce, on the southern coast, which is the greatest storehouse of the well-preserved houses and buildings which were built during the era of King Sugar and before (just one example is on the **previous page, lower right**); walking through the old sections of the city is like stepping back in time sixty or seventy years. I have a special fondness for Ponce, for I lived there for some months in 1969 while I did my training for service as a Volunteer in the Peace Corps. And so it was with great interest that I returned there for the first time—wondering whether "progress" had despoiled the city's historic center, and especially its beautiful Plaza de las Delicias.

But I need not have feared. Ponce had been in good hands during my absence, and has safeguarded the tradition express-ed in one of the city's mottos: "Ponce es Ponce" (Ponce is ((always)) Ponce). The tree-shaded plaza, with its fountain, statues, the red-and-black painted firehouse, and its cathedral (**this page**), seemed exactly as I remembered it. There was one noteworthy change: just across the street was a brand-new Burger King, whose construction had doubtless caused some consternation among those concerned for the preservation of the city's heritage—but they need not have worried, for the restaurant has been built in a design which blends beautifully into its setting.

In preserving the charm of its past Ponce has of course not had to contend with the enormous population and economic growth pressures that have beset the San Juan metropolitan area (and to a lesser extent much of the entire north coast). But Ponce has also been fortunate in having a nucleus of active and involved citizens—including members of such distinguished Ponce families as Serrallés, Mayoral, Sauri, and Mayol—who have given meaning to the city's nickname, "la Ciudad Señorial" (the term defies exact translation—an approximation would be 'the noble city'). But if any one family name has come to be associated with Ponce, it is that of Ferré.

I met the titular head of that family, Luis A. Ferré—indus-trialist, long-time member of the Puerto Rican Senate, and former Governor—in the city's pride and joy, and the crown-ing cultural achievement† of Don Luis's remarkably varied eighty years, the Ponce Museum of Art, which he built and donated to the city (shown **opposite page, lower left**, and in which Mr. Ferré is posed **opposite page, upper right** next to 'Cain and Abel,' by sculptor Jef Lambeaux). Founder of the

New Progressive Party, which carried him to the Governorship in 1968, Mr. Ferré is an ardent proponent of statehood for the island. "But today we'll talk of art, not politics," he admonished. "I think it's important that people know we have this sort of thing here." Then he led me on a brief tour of some of the outstanding pieces on display, including a giant canvas entitled 'El Velorio' (The Wake) by Puerto Rico's turn-of-the-century impressionist, Francisco Oller (1833-1917) and 18th-century works by portraitist José Campeche (1751-1809), considered to have been Puerto Rico's first outstanding artist.

Later that same day I would meet Don Luis's younger sister, Sor Isolina, a nun of the Missionary Servants of the Most Blessed Trinity order, whose list of honors and awards probably surpasses even that of her brother. Sister Isolina, as she is known to most people, spent most of her life with the order in the States, much of the time working in the barrios of New York City, before returning to Puerto Rico at the age of fifty-four "to take it a little easier." But apparently a slower pace was not in her nature, for shortly after her return she began

working with the youth in one of the city's poorest barrios, Playa de Ponce, and in 1969 founded the Centro de Orientación, which, as she put it, with a laugh, "Just grew!"

Today her Centro occupies an entire complex of buildings on land that was donated to the center, counts dozens of full-time and volunteer workers, and has provided training in a wide variety of disciplines, including home economics, photography, furniture making, and the arts, for thousands of young trainees. "I don't believe there are any 'naturally' bad people," she commented, "but without opportunities, without creative outlets, sometimes people feel they have no choices left—our real problem here in Puerto Rico is the lack of jobs."

It was a litany I was to hear repeated countless times during my months in Puerto Rico—and understandably so, for with an official unemployment rate which is routinely twice that of the mainland (and with claims that the true rate is even higher), unemployment is obviously a serious and pressing problem.

† In venturing this opinion I risk offending Mr. Ferré's considerable reputation as a pianist.

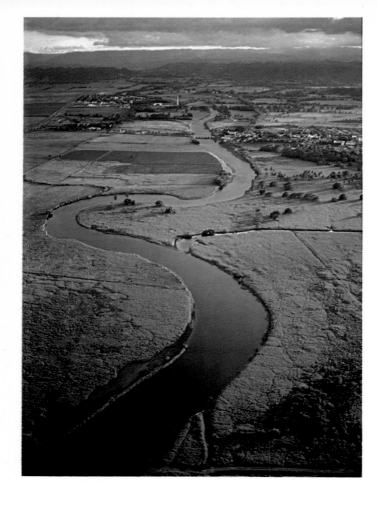

north)—all of which result in the northern coast being much more humid than the southern, and being generally cloudier and cooler (**this page, upper left**, an aerial view of the northern plain and the Río de la Plata near Dorado. (One consequence of this climatalogical difference is that the north coast was more heavily populated than the south in the early years of the island's settlement, a pattern which continues today.)

This additional rainfall on the northern plain permits the cultivation of crops which the southern climate will not support. One such crop is pineapple (shown being harvested on a government farm, **this page, lower right**), and a large area centered around Barceloneta is dedicated to its cultivation. In the recent past pineapple was a significant export for the island, but in recent years the entire crop has been sold in the local market.

Another government project is converting former cane land between Manatí and Arecibo to rice cultivation (**opposite page, lower left**, a cropduster applies herbicide to a recently-planted paddy), in an attempt to reduce the country's dependence on rice imported from Texas, Louisiana, and California.

Such projects are welcome attempts to reduce the island's dependence on imported food and at the same time provide jobs

*T*he region to the north of the Cordillera Central facing the Atlantic presents an entirely different aspect from that of the southern plain, both in topography and vegetation. Perhaps the most striking feature of the region is the karst formation—known in Puerto Rico as los mogotes—which occurs between the coastal lowlands and the foothills of the Cordillera, from San Juan westward almost to the west coast of the island. The lusher vegetation along the north coast results from a combination of factors: the generally northeasterly Caribbean trade winds, a slight southerly inclination of the Cordillera Central as it runs east, and the location of the island divide (closer to the Caribbean coast than the Atlantic, meaning that most of the island's rain falls and runs off out of the Cordillera toward the

for the unemployed, but it has long been recognized that with less than one-quarter acre of arable land per person, it is unrealistic to expect substantial improvements in the standard of living to come from increased agricultural production. Although the first four decades of the century brought significant improvements in the levels of health and education and to the island's infrastructure, in the mid-1940s Puerto Rico's per capita income was still below $200. It was during this period that a 'peaceful revolution' in the island's political structure took place, bringing to power the instigator of that revolution, Luis Muñoz Marín. Muñoz clearly saw that Puerto Rico could not remain an agricultural society if it was to pull itself out of the grinding poverty which had historically been the island's lot. With Muñoz's appointment of a young former pharmacist named Teodoro Moscoso to devise and direct an island-controlled industrial policy, the foundations for what would become "Operation Bootstrap," and its administering agency "Fomento" (formally, the Economic Development Administration) were laid.

The policy devised was based on a combination of tax incentives and the island's abundant low-cost labor to induce off-island (mainly American) companies to set up offshore manufacturing

operations in Puerto Rico. Consistent with the skill level of the labor supply, early efforts concentrated on attracting industries such as clothing and leather-goods manufacture (in the 1950s much of the world baseball production was sewn in Puerto Rico), and Fomento succeeded in attracting over 2500 manufacturing plants to the island, in the process creating more than 100,000 new industrial jobs. But the early strategy of seeking low-skill, low-value-added industries which brought such stunning success began running out of steam in the 1960s, owing to two developments: first, the rising standard of living in Puerto Rico—brought about in large part by the industrialization program itself—brought steady pressure for higher wages on the island, thus reducing the country's comparative wage advantage

(this process was exacerbated by the eventual extension of the federal minimum wage to Puerto Rico); and second, even lower-wage countries—many inspired by the Puerto Rican example—launched their own campaigns to lure the same type of manufacturing operations by setting up industrial free trade zones. (One nearby example is Haiti, where workers now sew the baseballs which Puerto Ricans made in the 1950s.)

Thus faced in the 1960s with the increasing difficulty of continuing to attract low-skill-level industries, Fomento shifted course, and began seeking "high-tech" firms requiring a more skilled labor force and providing in turn higher-value-added jobs. The strategy has been remarkably successful in attracting the pharmaceutical industry—by recent count nearly 90 drug firms were manufacturing on the island, including such household names as Upjohn, Eli Lilly, and Abbott Laboratories (at whose Barceloneta plant, **previous page, upper right** a worker in a "clean" room operates machinery making Ogen, an estrogen-based drug, just one of a number of products manufactured at the facility. At another nearby plant, the Swiss pharmaceutical giant Hoffmann-La Roche makes its entire U.S. production of Valium.)

Near Caguas I visited the plants of another industry that Fomento has been successful in enticing to the island, computer manufacturing. The maker of small business computers, MDS Qantel came to Puerto Rico in 1978 (**this page, top** a worker performs a final brightness level test on the computer before it is boxed for shipment). The company was lured to the island, General Manager Nick Ramos told me, by the tax incentives offered—in Qantel's case, a tax holiday of 15 years (the duration of the exemption varies from 10 to 25 years, depending on the location of the plant, to encourage plants to locate in areas of highest unemployment). "But once we were here, we realized that the quality of the workers was another big plus—this is a very cost-effective plant. And all of our workers here—including the engineers, are Puerto Rican. Me, I was born in New York but raised in San Juan, so I guess I'm the reverse of a 'Neorican'!" His pride in the plant and work force was obvious as he ticked off the plant's accomplishments: one of the fastest plant start-up times ever, the first computer memory totally developed—by Puerto Ricans engineers—in Puerto Rico (of which there have been only two field failures among the 10,000 units the plant has manufactured). It was an impressive recital.

Lord and Taylor on the mainland, as well as in shops in Puerto Rico. Specializing in sequined and beaded evening gowns, Mrs. Alfaro's original creations have commanded prices of up to $10,000. But, by her own account, her proudest achievement is the seamstress school she founded and supervises, and where she personally teaches techniques which enable women to easily make their own clothes without commercial patterns.

Far removed from San Juan, and as far removed from high fashion as one could imagine, a Star-Kist canning plant in Mayagüez packs and ships half a billion cans of tuna annually (**this page, lower right**), and is the island's largest employer under one roof. As is the case with the island's other four canneries, Star-Kist's tuna comes from fishing grounds in virtually all the world's oceans, although, ironically, not from near Puerto Rico.

At a plant nearby another company, Columbia Data Products, also produces small business computers with an all-Puerto Rican work force—and with one additional distinction: its chairman, founder, and major shareholder, William Díaz (**opposite page, bottom**) is also Puerto Rican. The company produces its model 1600-4 Multi-Personal Computer, considered one of the industry's leading IBM-compatible computers, at both the Puerto Rico plant and at company headquarters in Maryland, and has plans for a third plant in Ireland. A stock issue which took the company public in early 1984 made Mr. Díaz one of the wealthiest Puerto Ricans anywhere.

While the island has been losing its labor-intensive industries such as textile and apparel manufacturing to lower-wage countries, the reputation of its clothing designers has been steadily growing, and the labels of Puerto Rican designers like Nono Maldonado, Mili Arango, Fernando Pena, and Carlota Alfaro (in red dress, **this page, upper left** in the cutting room of her workshop in San Juan) are increasingly seen in boutiques and department stores like Bonwit-Teller, Sak's Fifth Avenue, and

*T*he fishing that is done in Puerto Rico's coastal waters and bays (as **opposite**, where a pair of fishermen cast into the waters of Arecibo Bay at sunset) is limited to small inboards and outboards like the one in which I accompanied 54-year-old Pepe González (**this page**) on a weekly check of his 12 fish pots (wire mesh traps) set on the deep reef off Arecibo.

I joined Pepe in the predawn darkness at his 18-foot yola tied to the fishermen's association dock in Islote. (While Puerto Ricans have traditionally been prodigious consumers of fish, the great bulk of it has been in the form of dried salt cod imported from Newfoundland and Norway. Some years ago the government built the association's facility as part of an island-wide program aimed at increasing the supply of fresh fish reaching the market. While the program achieved some success, locally-caught fish remain a tiny percentage of total fish consumption.) With a pull or two, the 18-horsepower Evinrude sputtered to life and we were on our way out the channel, through Arecibo Bay, and onto the sea, still calm as the sun rose through the horizon.

"I've been fishing since I was eight years old," he remarked, in answer to my question. Not "full-time" (using the English expression) though—I worked for 29 years as a maintenance man in the Central Cambalache before it shut down a couple years back. I had to do something, and I'd always done a little fishing on the side, so I decided to be a fisherman for a living—I've got a family to feed." We were approaching the first of his pots, marked by a red plastic buoy, and Pepe cut the outboard and fired up a gasoline-powered winch to haul the 80-pound pot the 100 feet to the surface. It was a disappointing catch: a few small fish, which he threw back, and a couple of slightly larger colorado which he tossed into the bottom of the boat. I expressed surprise that he would keep fish that small. "Well, that's mostly what we get now—if I don't keep those, I wouldn't get hardly anything at all." And with a selling price of $2.50 a pound, he can hardly afford to throw away even one-pounders.

The rest of the morning would pass much the same way, and after hauling six more pots, Pepe decided to call it a day, and we headed home. "I'll come back in a few days," he remarked ruefully. "Looks like there haven't been many fish this week."

Pepe's poor catch came as no great surprise, for he has seen the coastal fishing slowly decline over his lifetime—ironically, that very government fishing program that built the fishermen's association dock has contributed to that decline by putting more working fishermen on the water.

"New" San Juan

*B*ursting at the seams, metropolitan San Juan *spreads ever outward, as seen in this aerial view over the western edge of the city. The metropolitan area has tripled in population during the past 40 years (today counting well over 1,000,000 inhabitants), and has mushroomed in size. Today roughly one in every three island residents lives in "San Juan." (Just what is 'San Juan,' of course, depends on your point of reference: to the outsider, San Juan is likely to be the continuous urban concentration radiating out from San Juan Bay in all directions, including the cities of Bayamón—which alone counts 200,000 residents—to the west, and Carolina—another 165,000—to the southeast. To the traditionalist, it is "Viejo San Juan," the area within the stone walls built around the old city in the seventeenth century. In strict terms, it is the area shown in yellow on the map* **overleaf,** *which contained some 435,000 inhabitants in 1980. Interestingly, that area itself has remained relatively stable in population for the past two decades: population growth in the capital has occurred primarily by spreading out, not up, and by "filling in" the areas between older population centers. Since, for artistic considerations I have left the treatment of the old city to the end of this book, I have, for want of a better expression, coined the term "New San Juan" to label the city outside the ancient walls. As Puerto Ricans well know, it is not a term in general use, and, to those who may be offended, my apologies.)*

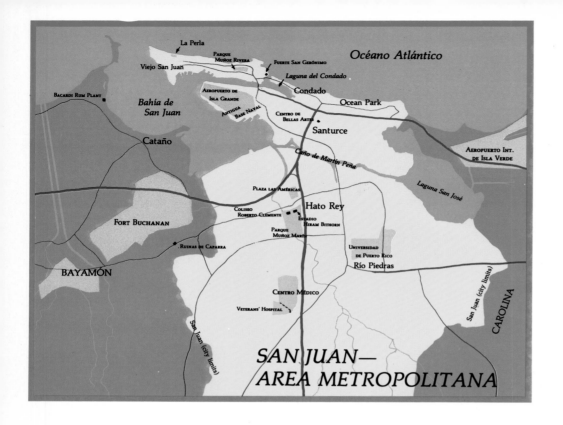

SAN JUAN—
AREA METROPOLITANA

would have fit in anywhere in my native California. *(San Juan's Plaza las Américas, **this page, lower right**, is rumored to be the busiest shopping center in the world, a claim which, though difficult to verify, is believable after a visit on a Friday or Saturday afternoon. Whether intentional or not, the center's name seems especially appropriate at such times, for, judging from the amount of socializing going on, the center fills the role played by the central plaza of the island's smaller towns, a feature of small-town life sadly lost in the urban sprawl of the capital city.)*

Despite a history which makes it the oldest European city under the American flag, the newer areas of San Juan have a look as modern as any on the mainland (**opposite**, a view of the financial district in Hato Rey).

One of my bigger surprises in getting to know Puerto Rico was the discovery of supermarkets and shopping centers in San Juan which, save for the language factor,

*I*t was not until the turn of the century that San Juan's growth began pushing beyond the stone walls of the Old City (the eastern edge of the city was the Santiago gate, near today's Plaza de Colón; only in 1897, after consultation with Spanish military authorities, who doubtless advised that the 17th-century walls had outlived their original purpose, was the southeastern section of the wall torn down to make way for commercial expansion). The city would then spread down San Juan Island, and onto the "mainland," the area of San Juan now known generally as Santurce. Originally planned as an exclusive residential zone, the area known as "the Condado" (**this page**, in an aerial view looking eastward), would receive a big boost to its development with the construction of the Dos Hermanos Bridge (named for its builders, ITT pioneer Sosthenes Behn and his brother Hernand, who were the owners of much of the property in the Condado).

But the exclusivity originally intended for the Condado, though still visible on its tree-shaded streets and in many of the large houses which were built in the first decades of the century (such as this impressive Spanish-style, **opposite, upper left**), was to be relatively short-lived. In the 1950s, the same long-distance airliners that

tioners and local residents, the latter searching for an alternative to fighting the capital's streets, being increasingly overwhelmed by the automobile explosion of the post-war period. That change in 'atmosphere' in the Condado, and the recent spurt in the crime rate, which has affected the whole island, give added meaning to the decorative grillwork (**this page, lower right**) which adorns nearly all houses in the island's urban areas, and, increasingly, in the campo as well.

---

†The immediate and phenomenal success of the island's first deluxe "tourist" hotel, the Caribe Hilton, which opened in 1949, did much to demonstrate the island's potential for attracting the developing winter-season tourist market. When first planned, the uncertainty of the market made it necessary for the government to build the hotel, which was then leased to the Hilton chain—its first venture outside the Continental U.S.

were carrying emigrating Puerto Ricans north to new lives in and around New York City began carrying winter-weary northerners south to the island's sun and sand.†

The island's tourism industry was born, and grew steadily over the next two and a half decades (receiving a big boost when the deterioration of Cuban-American relations after 1960 led to the closing of Cuba as an American tourist destination). The Condado and the adjoining areas all the way to Isla Verde became known as Puerto Rico's "gold coast" as hotel after hotel opened to the ever-growing waves of tourists.

Not surprisingly, the influx of tourist-oriented businesses—including fast-food restaurants, curio shops and the like—meant the end of the Condado as a quiet, exclusive and genteel neighborhood. Adding to the change in atmosphere in the '60s and '70s was the sprouting of condominiums to house both the vaca-

of the most expensive in the Caribbean, and added to a serious "image" problem both among the general tourist public as well as with travel professionals. ("Our trouble," one taxi driver told me, "is that Puerto Rico doesn't really need tourism, like the other islands do. On those other islands, if the tourists don't come, they don't have anything at all to live on. But people here know that if the tourists don't come, there's always something else to fall back on—and that affects people's attitudes.") The fact of labor strife on the island is hardly a new phenomenon, for Puerto Rico has had a strong labor union movement since early in this century. (One of the "Fifty Years Ago Today" articles to appear in a San Juan newspaper during my stay related the story of a strike by sugar workers at Central Aguirre in 1934.)

The decline in the tourist industry's fortunes has inevitably had its impact along the hotel row of the Condado and Isla Verde, as revenues and property values have declined. The area has clearly seen better days: "Sloppy Joe's—World Famous Meeting Place, Open 24 Hours" now stands boarded up, as do a number of its

The tourism boom which built the hotels and condominiums along the "gold coast" began to falter in the late '70s, however, leading to a number of hotel closings (as **this page, upper left**). A variety of factors, including the repeated worldwide economic reverses beginning in 1973, were undoubtedly at work. Still another factor was the rise in the '60s and '70s of other Caribbean tourist destinations, which had taken a lesson from Puerto Rico's early and striking success. More disturbing, perhaps, has been the role of local factors such as labor costs and disputes (**this page, lower right**, the employees of a car rental agency on the picket line near the airport entrance during the winter season of 1984), which have helped make the island one

neighbors along Ashford Avenue, the Condado's main thoroughfare ("San Juan's Champs Elysées," one enthusiastic guide book terms it), and visitors and residents alike must now seek a less-famous spot for their rendezvous.

There are hopeful signs, however: there are indications that labor, aware of the competition posed by other tourist destinations and sobered by the loss of jobs from numerous hotel closings (or conversions to condominiums), have moderated their wage demands and become increasingly productivity-conscious, all of which is encouraging for hotel prices. Hotel owners, for their part, have been refurbishing their properties and revamped their advertising campaigns to try to sell Puerto Rico as an entire island, with more to offer than just beaches. With the closing of marginal hotels, they have reason to hope that a slimmed-down industry will be in a better competitive position. (During my stay in the winter of 1983-84, a number of hotels were in fact operating at or near full occupancy.) Another encouraging sign is the remodeling and opening of a number of other businesses in the Condado area (such as the converted 1940s mansion, **previous page**, housing a deluxe restaurant and high-fashion salon, among other busnesses), which is doing much to improve the atmosphere in the area.

Despite the tremendous expansion of the city over the past decades, and despite the problems which the headlong rush into the industrial (and automobile) age has brought, San Juan remains a highly liveable city. Clearly near the top of the list of attractions is the island's year-round summerlike weather, and the city's location on the ocean, which enables it to be taken full advantage of. No point in the city is more than 20 minutes from the water, whether that be miles of open—and all public—beach, or the protected Condado Lagoon (**this page**), a favorite with windsurfers, boaters, bridge-side fishermen, and those simply wanting to "take the air." And, despite the proximity of the campo in the other direction, the city is blessed with a large amount of "green space" within its boundaries, including Luis Muñoz Rivera Park in Puerta de Tierra (**opposite**), where a father can take his son for a quiet bicycle ride.

*T*raffic streams out of the city along one of its modern expressways as evening falls (**this page**). Certainly the most visible symbol of the rise of the island's middle class in the post-World War II era, the ubiquitous automobile† has transformed living patterns, especially in the capital, where the near-constant *tapones* (traffic jams) must be contended with on a daily basis.

The use of the private car has, of course, been indispensable to the growth of the capital's suburbs, and has generally contributed to the "Americanization" of the society's lifestyle. Unlike the usual pattern four decades ago, most of the capital's residents now go to a work place far removed from their homes, and seldom live in close proximity to their fellow workers. This fact, coupled with the high degree of sociability characteristic of Puerto Ricans, has given great impetus to the custom of "Viernes Social" (Social Friday)—the traditional get-together with fellow workers and friends at the end of the workweek—an event which can stretch into the late hours of the evening (as **opposite**, at an all-night, open-air eatery in Santurce. So well-honored is the custom that the Friday evening rush-hour traffic out of the city is noticeably lighter than on other workdays.)

For workers at the container port on San Juan Bay (**this page, lower**), however, evening brings no slackening of the workpace if a ship is alongside. San Juan remains by far the island's leading general merchandise port, and with the great bulk of the island's consumption items—including over half of its food—being met by imports, its role is obviously crucial. (In 1974 the Commonwealth government, concerned with the costs and reliability of its vital ocean shipping, acquired its own merchant container fleet, which it continues to operate in competition with numerous private lines. Virtually all the island's general merchandise is today containerized.)

---

† *The number of private cars zoomed from 37,000 in 1951 to over 900,000 in 1980, making Puerto Rico, considered as a separate country, sixth in the world in per-capita car ownership.*

*I*t would be misleading to conclude from the phenomenal development of the economy and the middle class in the post-war period that the poverty which once afflicted Puerto Rico like a scourge is altogether a thing of the past. (Indeed, one of the sharpest criticisms of the island's present tax and economic structure is that the distribution of income and wealth in the society has become less equitable in the past two decades.) It is certainly true that the abysmal conditions which prevailed at the turn of the century and, to a lessening degree, into the forties, have disappeared, thanks to the country's industrialization program and the more recent extension of welfare programs to the very poor.

Nonetheless the slums that came to be an infamous feature of the city during the forties can still be found. Undoubtedly the most studied and most famous of these is La Perla (**this page**), huddled on San Juan Island between the Old City's walls and the Atlantic Ocean. La Perla gained nationwide notoriety in 1965 with the publication of La Vida, a book by the American sociologist Oscar Lewis, based on his extended study of families in the community. Though far from the worst of San Juan's arrabales, La Perla thus came to symbolize slum conditions in the capital. Those conditions, in La Perla as well as the other slum areas of the city, are today greatly improved—the vast majority of the shanties have electricity and running water, and even television sets and refrigerators. But many of La Perla's residents remain bitter about Lewis's depiction of their barrio. I chatted early one morning with a couple of La Perlans at the domino tables installed among the palms next to the city wall. "Where Mr. Lewis went wrong," commented one, "was in the family he chose to study about. It was weeks into the study before the man even realized that he had chosen a family that was mostly prostitutes— and by that point he didn't want to throw out all that research. So he just went on ahead, and published a book about La Perla based mostly on a family of prostitutes! Now there are prostitutes here in La Perla, true, but most families here are normal working people—those who can get work. Of course we were mad! Who wouldn't be?!"

Certainly La Perla today, seen up close, does not appear the den of iniquity suggested by La Vida; doubtless there have been many changes in the two decades since the study was conducted. Indeed, in many ways today La Perla seems more a lower-middle-class area—albeit rundown—than a slum in the popular sense. Most of the buildings are substantial, concrete-block structures, many with air conditioners, and at any one time there are dozens being improved or added to by their owners. And a plethora of free services—including a federal Head Start program, a municipal multiple-services center for the elderly (offering low-cost meals and medical care), and a day-care center (**this page, upper**) tend to the needs of La Perla's residents.

One problem that does exist in La Perla, as it does throughout the island, is the problem of drug addiction. Indeed, with an estimated 30,000 heroin addicts alone, the island has one of the highest addiction rates in the U.S. On the outskirts of Río Piedras I learned of a unique, island-born program called Hogar Crea which is meeting with extraordinary success in helping addicts. Founded in 1968 by an ex-addict who felt that only those who had "been there" could help the addict to help himself, the program uses intensive group counseling and self-criticism—all directed by ex-addicts—to encourage its 'clients' to face up to the root causes of their dependency (**this page, lower**, a counselor and clients hold an informal rap session in one of the home's dormitories). The program stresses the need for its residents to 're-educate' themselves in essential life-skills, on the theory that it was the failure to acquire them in the first place that led to the addiction. The program's course may take a client as long as three years to complete; to date over a thousand have successfully done so. Encouraged by this record, private and public funding have helped the program to expand island-wide to over 60 facilities, which were treating over 5000 addicts in 1983.

Today

The father of modern Puerto Rico, Luis Muñoz Marín, becomes the subject of a history lesson between mother and daughter viewing his portrait on temporary display in the the Ponce Museum of Art (**this page**). Born just months before the American invasion of 1898, he matured with the century, and wrought a transformation of Puerto Rico's politics and economy so profound that it touched every aspect of Puerto Rican life. At his death in May of 1980 all Puerto Rico mourned, for it knew that a giant had passed from among them.

The son of Luis Muñoz Rivera, the newspaper publisher-turned-political leader who had struggled in the closing decade of the 19th century for the island's autonomy under Spain (only to see the dream of self-rule evaporate under America's handling of her new possession), Muñoz Marín in the first part of his life gave no outward indication of the role he was to eventually play in Puerto Rico's history. Most of his formative years were spent in the States, where he would pass his early manhood as a writer. (Although his writings were predominantly political essays or journalistic pieces, his occasional forays into poetry would earn him his life-long nickname, "El Vate"—"the Poet.") Thus when he returned to the island to live in 1931, to many of the people who had expected a great political career for Muñoz Rivera's son, he seemed a bit of a dilettante. But even in his years away from the island the young Muñoz was gaining a perspective on Puerto Rico and its problems (indeed many of his writings had dealt with those very issues); and, perhaps equally important, on the nature and workings of the American nation, perspectives which would have been impossible to achieve from within the island. And so when Muñoz came back to Puerto Rico for good at the age of 33, he knew his own mind, and he knew what had to be done if Puerto Rico was to lose its notorious epithet, "the Poorhouse of the Caribbean."

Although America's rule over its colony had eventually established a limited democratic framework for self-rule in most local matters (the presidentially-appointed governor retained a broad veto power), the rise of the great sugar interests had severely compromised the island's political processes. In the late 1930s, amidst the island's grinding poverty, it remained common for people—especially in the rural areas—to sell their votes ($5.00, or a pair of shoes, was the normal price). Under these conditions, the island's government was obviously powerless to effect any change in the economic or social structure which might threaten powerful vested interests.

Into this situation Muñoz moved decisively, launching in 1938 a grassroots political campaign in the countryside unlike anything Puerto Rico had ever seen. His strategy was disarmingly simple: faced with the impossible task of out-bidding the entrenched economic interests in a vote-buying war, Muñoz instead asked the jíbaros to "lend" him their votes—with the "loans" to be repaid in the form of real change and economic progress. In a strenuous campaign that took him to every corner of the island, Muñoz won the jíbaros' confidence—and their votes. With the 1940 election Muñoz and his Populares won effective control of the island's legislature from the sugar interests, thus positioning themselves to institute the economic programs which have been discussed earlier (**see** "Island"). Thus in the space of two years and with a bold political strategy Muñoz had started Puerto Rico on its climb out of near-feudal conditions toward a modern,

democratic society. (In the next elections four years later Muñoz and his party would consolidate their control of the legislature with an overwhelming victory; and four years after that, in 1948, Muñoz would become the first governor of the island to be elected by the Puerto Rican people. Muñoz and his Populares would remain continuously in power until the elections of 1968.)

*L*uis Muñoz Marín succeeded in lifting Puerto Rico out of the dire economic straits which had shackled the island since its beginnings, and he came to believe that Puerto Rico could best serve her people with local autonomy, or as a "free associated state" within the American nation (a relationship which would be formalized with the adoption of the Puerto Rican Constitution in 1952); but even he was not able to put an end to the debate which had dominated public discussion since the turn of the century, as it continues to do today.

The issue is summarized in one word: 'status'—and in Puerto Rico that word refers to the political relationship between the mainland and the island. Indeed, with the vast improvement in

combo warms up a group of Independentistas *before the party's 1983 nominating convention); the pro-commonwealth Popular Democratic Party* (**opposite page, top right** *a caravan of Populares campaigns through the countryside near Peñuelas); the pro-statehood New Progressive Party* (**this page, top left** *an enthusiastic group of Novoprogresistas cheer on a speaker at a campaign rally); and a second pro-statehood party formed in 1983, the Puerto Rican Renewal Party. (Traditionally, each of the island's parties has been identified with its own symbol and color; when they organized in 1983 the Renovacionistas, finding all the best colors already taken, hit on the idea of a rainbow as their party symbol,* **this page, lower right**, *which resolved the color dilemma and fit in well with their theme of bringing together diverse viewpoints into one party).* †

---

† *Since the 1952 election (when it polled nearly 20 per cent), the pro-independence vote has dwindled to a very small share, with the pro-commonwealth and pro-statehood parties roughly splitting about 95 per cent of the ballots. In a 1967 plebiscite on the status question the Independence Party refused to participate, urging abstention. Commonwealth status was favored by 60.5 per cent of those voting, while 38.9 per cent voted in favor of statehood.*

the standard of living for the island since the Second World War, that debate has, if anything, become all the more acute, as economic concerns have become relatively less so. "In this country," a Puerto Rican acquaintance advised me, "everything is politics; and politics means the status issue." (Although the word is not found in standard Spanish-language dictionaries, in Puerto Rico it has become part and parcel of the Spanish lexicon.)

Status is the issue on which every Puerto Rican has an opinion, whether expressed or not, and it is the issue which divides and indentifies the island's political parties (which are unique to Puerto Rico, and only loosely affiliated—if at all—with any of the mainland's national parties). Simply put, there are three basic positions on the status issue: 1) independence, 2) continuation of the present commonwealth relationship with the U.S., and 3) statehood within the United States.

The status issue is so complex that an entire book would be required to treat it properly, and no attempt will be made to even approach it here. Suffice to say that, at this writing (in the midst of the island's 1984 election campaign) there were four parties likely to gain five per cent or more of the vote: the Puerto Rican Independence Party (**opposite page, bottom left** *an impromptu*

*N*o issue so charges the status debate as does the concern over the preservation of the country's cultural identity.† Given the economic and demographic developments of the past decades (in 1900 only 15 per cent of the population was classified as urban, while today that figure stands at 70 per cent), it is hardly surprising that the island has experienced profound cultural evolution. A more sensitive source of this change, however, has been the nearly ninety years of association with the United States—first as a colony, then more recently (with the Commonwealth), under local autonomy—which has inevitably meant the absorption of many aspects of American culture, of which English words, American pop music, and American fast-food are only the most visible aspects. This cultural "invasion" has given rise to a justifiably strong concern for the preservation of the island's cultural heritage.‡

Thus it is especially heartening to see the strong support Puerto Ricans give to the island's traditional cultural expression, both as participants and as spectators. Among the more colorful are the many shows and contests of Paso Fino horses (the term means "fine gaited"; **this page**, a contestant shows a yearling in an annual show which will determine the breed's island-wide champions), the refined descendants of the horses the Spanish brought to the colony in its early centuries, and which proved so suited to the island's mountainous interior.

Some months later I attended a standing-room-only performance of Areyto (**opposite**), the island's oldest and best-known folkloric group, and joined in the thunderous applause as they danced and sang their way through numbers representing diverse elements of the island's culture, including the Spanish colonial era, the jíbaro, and the vejigantes of Ponce and Loíza.

† *In using the term "country" to refer to the island, the knowledgeable will understand that I am not making a political statement, but merely adopting the custom of Puerto Ricans themselves—including Statehooders—of using the term to refer to Puerto Rico. The practice has something to do with linguistic habit and idiosyncracy (the Spanish term país has less of a political connotation than does its English translation), and something to do with the very pride of cultural identity here being discussed.*
‡ *The issue of cultural preservation is an especially sensitive one in view of the first decades of American administration of the island, when a concerted and heavy-handed attempt was made to "Americanize" the Puerto Rican people. One of the techniques most resented, and least effective, was the insistence on the use of English as the sole language of instruction in all schools on the island. Since Puerto Ricans at that time had otherwise had very little contact with English, one can imagine the results. The attempt was soon dropped, but various other schemes to make English the first language of the schools continued into the 1940s.*

ing programs: teaching the traditional musical in-
struments of the island.

*After shooting some photographs of a novice class on
the ground floor* (**this page, upper left**), *I caught the
strains of a familiar melody coming from above, and
found my way to the second-floor level. And then for
the next half hour I put my cameras aside and simply
listened, enchanted, while an advanced class trilled its
way through repeated renditions of its project for the
week, the haunting, melancholic theme song of the city,
"En Mi Viejo San Juan."*

*San Juan's cultural offerings are hardly limited to the
island's traditional culture: a symphony orchestra
(originally organized by the late, renowned cellist Pablo
Casals), several legitimate theatre groups, and various
resident ballet companies provide regular offerings
(including "Swan Lake,"* **this page, lower right**, *which I
photographed in rehearsal by the Ballet de San Juan
troup).*

*In the field of painting, Francisco Rodón has gained
an international reputation with his superbly expressive*

*T*he economic development which has inevitably
brought changes to the island's traditional culture has also, however, made it economically
possible to support efforts to preserve that culture (and
paradoxically, doubtless heightened public interest in
doing so). Thus it was that I found myself one Saturday
morning at the historic Convento de los Domínicos (**see
"Mi Viejo San Juan"**), headquarters of the Institute of
Puerto Rican Culture, whose mission it is to work to
preserve and promote the island's cultural heritage. The
courtyard of the building resounded with the cacophany
of some 200 cuatros playing different melodies. The
musicians, ranging in age from 12 to 60, were all participants in one of the Instituto's most popular continu-

portraits of such figures as Rómulo Betancourt, Jorge Luis Borges, and Alicia Alonso (Mr. Rodón is seen **this page, upper right** with his painting of Philippe de Montebello, Director of New York's Metropolitan Museum); in Puerto Rico unquestionably his best-known work is the portrait of Luis Muñoz Marín, seen in the opening photograph of this section.

But it is undoubtedly in the field of the lithographic arts that the reputation of Puerto Rican artists has spread more than in any other. Producing silk-screen prints and posters with bold, innovative designs, the work of artists like Rafael Tufiño, Jose Alicea, and Lorenzo Homar have become known far beyond the island. I met the latter at his studio in Río Piedras (**this page, lower left**), toward the end of my stay in Puerto Rico. It was one of those all-too-rare experiences which make my line of work fascinating: pressed for time by a project he was trying to finish, Mr. Homar had granted me twenty minutes for a photo session. But Lorenzo Homar the raconteur won out over Lorenzo Homar the artist: I ended up spending all morning in his studio,

listening to his stories of service in the Pacific with the U.S. Army during World War II, of his years as head of the Graphic Arts Workshop at the Institute of Puerto Rican Culture, of his early and continuing passion for gymnastics, and of the problems and triumphs of one of Puerto Rico's premier artists practicing his art on a small tropical island. (Ever the innovator, and no slave to convention, he shocked traditionalists by switching to Mylar in preference to paper as the medium for his silkscreen designs, finding it ideally suited to withstanding the tropical humidity which quickly ruins paper lithographs.) It was a morning which passed like a moment, and soon it was I who had to go; I left with the hope that our paths will cross again, for such people are rare finds indeed.

A rising standard of living has also made possible the leisure time for sports, and the sight of men and boys in baseball uniforms heading for a weekend game (like the one I photographed in Jayuya, **opposite**) is a common one. Undoubtedly the island's greatest sports legend is Roberto Clemente, the baseball player who died tragically in an airplane crash while accompanying a shipment of relief supplies to earthquake-ravished Nicaragua in 1972. He is memorialized today in various forms throughout the island—the covered sports arena in San Juan is named for him—including a mural decorating the wall of a building in Clemente's hometown, Carolina (**this page**).

Puerto Ricans also compete in their own delegations, under their own flag, in international sporting competitions (including the Olympics, where they also have the option of competing with the United States team, as some have done). After baseball, probably the island's most popular sport in the spectator sense is boxing, due in part to the fact that Puerto Ricans, including Sixto Escobar, Carlos Ortiz, and Wilfredo Benítez, have at various times held some fifteen world titles.

It is of course as a tropical isle, her "sun, sand, and sea" that outsiders most think of when they visualize Puerto Rico, and her beaches (as near Patillas **opposite**), *are, to repeat a tired cliché, among the world's finest. And during "winter," outside the capital, virtually empty as well. For despite my doubts, it remains largely true that "Puerto Ricans don't go to the beach in winter," as I had read in an old* National Geographic *article. My visits to Luquillo, the most famous beach on the island, on February weekends revealed a parking lot one-tenth full, and the sands occupied principally by vacationing Continentals and visting Neoricans, all escaping the northern cold.*

*Sailing, motor boating, and deep-sea fishing (Puerto Rico is known as the "Capital of the Blue Marlin" for the size and number of the fish which have been taken off its shores) have a more constant following, and the island is a favorite stopping place for small craft sailing from the continent to the Lesser Antilles (***this page***, a visiting sailboat rocks on a gentle swell at sunrise near Fajardo).*

*I*n a Ciales classroom fifth-graders at the Horace Mann school hear a lesson on the origins of the Commonwealth and its flag (**this page**).

Since Puerto Rico was part of Spain until 1898, her people were Spanish citizens when the island was ceded to the United States under the Treaty of Paris which formally ended the Spanish-American War. The island then became "unincorporated territory" of the United States, and for the following 19 years the inhabitants of the island were "citizens of Porto Rico, under the protection of the United States." In 1917 the U.S. Congress—motivated in part by wanting to ensure Puerto Rican loyalty during World War I—passed the Jones Act, conferring U.S. citizenship on all Puerto Ricans who accepted it (something less than 300 people out of the population of 1.3 million declined).

Today, generally speaking, Puerto Ricans resident on the island have all the rights, privileges and duties of any U.S. citizen, with two principal exceptions: they have no vote in presidential and congressional elections (Puerto Rico is represented before the U.S. House of Representatives by an elected Resident Commissioner who has a voice in deliberations, but no vote, in Congress), and they pay no federal taxes on island-generated income. (A Puerto Rican who moves to the mainland automatically acquires the same rights, privileges and duties as any other Stateside citizen.)

On another visit to a rural school in the Ciales district I watched and listened as another class struggled through its English lesson for the day (**opposite page, upper**; all schoolchildren through the high school level take English as a mandatory subject). Later, between classes I chatted with one of the school's teachers: "English is a problem for us," he said with a sigh. "Few of our teachers are native English speakers, so the English the kids learn to speak isn't very good—you really can't teach a language in an hour a day anyway. But that hour a day robs time from other subjects the children need as much or more; so they fall behind the averages all around. It's a big problem."

Indeed, English has been a problem for Puerto Rico since the American invasion brought a colonial power of another tongue to the island. The efforts at "Americanization," including the attempt to make English the language of the school system, have been alluded to earlier.† In reading the history of the first decades of American administration of the island, it is hard to escape the conclusion that, even apart from those Americanization efforts, the language barrier—coupled with American attitudes about the "natural supremacy" of English—was a big factor in the continuing clashes between American administrators and Puerto Rican officials.

Today, with the control of the island's local and internal affairs firmly in the hands of elected Puerto Rican officials (a power transfer which evolved over the first half of this century, and which the promulgation of the Commonwealth's Constitution completed and formalized in 1952), tensions between Puerto Rican and U.S. officialdom are largely a thing of the past, although occasional clashes still occur, just as they do on the mainland, when federal law affects local matters.

But it would be misleading to conclude that the "language problem" has disappeared. Many critics view with concern the creeping invasion of English into the culture, often creating a mixture, in speech as well as in writing, of Spanish and English nicknamed "Spanglish" (as on a sign for a fast-food restaurant, **this page, lower**). One manifestation of this concern which occurred during my stay on the island: protesters picketed the performance of an English-language play being sponsored by the Institute of Puerto Rican Culture. And yet, despite the concern illustrated by such protests, my own experience was that most people were genuinely proud of their English-speaking ability: although I speak a

---

† *The Americanization even reached the point of changing the spelling of the island's name—presumably to accomodate its pronunciation by English speakers—to "Porto Rico" from 1900 to 1932.*

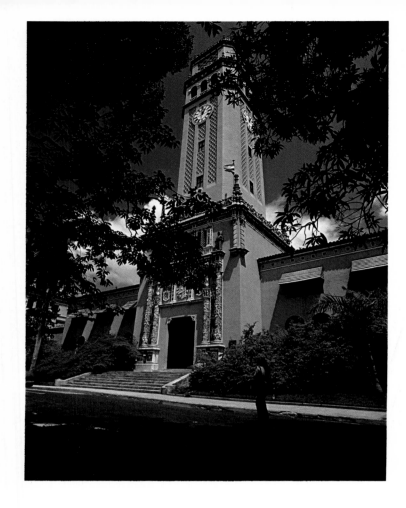

languages—principally Schweizerdeutch—for over 150 years; has uncomplainingly absorbed a good number of those convenient and German-sounding words, and yet remains distinctly—and proudly—Francophone to this day.).

*F*or years the Río Piedras campus of the University of Puerto Rico **(this page, upper left)** has been at the center of efforts to preserve the island's cultural identity—and the hotbed of support for the island's independence movement as well. During the sixties and seventies the campus was repeatedly shaken by protests—often with subcurrents of anti-Yanqui sentiment—which, like the protests on mainland campuses in that era, occasionally resulted in serious violence. Today, again like mainland universities, the campus is quieter, and the students' attention is more likely to be directed toward study and acquiring the practical skills that will be needed after graduation. (One indication of

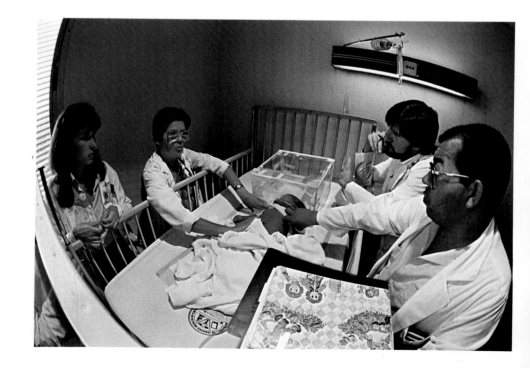

very good Spanish, having lived for five years in the neighboring Dominican Republic, I often found it difficult to carry on a Spanish conversation, simply because more often than not my interlocutor spoke English quite well (very often from having lived in the States), and was eager to practice it.

Despite these linguistic inroads, which are especially pronounced in the world of commerce and business, the language of the island clearly remains Spanish, and is unlikely to ever be any other, even while much of the population increasingly becomes bilingual. (After all, the canton and city of Geneva, Switzerland, where I lived for a time, has been similarly "invaded" by other

the shifting mood is the fact that the most recent protest violence was sparked by a rise in tuition fees, rather than a political issue.)

The University is relatively young, not having been founded until 1903, but it has grown into an enormous institution, with an enrollment today of over 50,000 students, spread over a number of facilities, including a major campus in Mayagüez. Schools of law, public administration, architecture, dentistry, and medicine, among others, provide the opportunity for specialized studies, in addition to the general science and humanities curriculum offered by the various undergraduate departments (**opposite page, lower right**, students in the Faculty of Medicine review a case with a professor in the pediatrics ward of the Centro Médico, the island's largest hospital).

Despite the University's tremendous expansion in recent years, it has been unable to satisfy the enormous demand for university-level education created by the island's explosive growth in population and its rapid drive toward industrialization. A number of other universities have sprung up to meet the need, but for those lucky enough to gain entrance (like the student, **this page**, prepping for a class on the Río Piedras campus), the University of Puerto Rico is felt to offer the broadest and highest quality education on the island.

(The young women studies under a monument to Puerto Rico's Eugenio María de Hostos, the writer, philosopher, and social thinker of the 19th century who remains among the outstanding figures of the island's history. He was an early advocate for the abolition of slavery, and for independence from Spain, as part of a federation of the West Indian islands. Hostos is known throughout Latin America for the ideas he contributed to progressive education.)

radio telescope has added to the knowledge of pulsars and quasars, to list but two of the "objects" which the observatory explores), but it is the sheer size of the dish and the "feed support structure" suspended overhead which most overwhelms the layman (the facility is open to visitors on Sunday afternoons).

Garred Giles, the facility's official greeter, showed me around: "It's hard for the non-specialist to relate to our activity here," he commented, as we rode a motorized cage out to the 600-ton feed support structure positioned by massive cables some 50 stories above the dish. "Probably what most impresses the general public is our 'Arecibo Message'—a coded radar signal we beamed out to the star cluster M-13, in Hercules. It had an effective beam power over 100 times as powerful as all the electric generating plants on earth. If there's any intelligent life out there, this message had about the best chance of letting them know someone's here."

Nestled among the mogotes south of Arecibo is a structure at once startling in its setting and at the same time symbolic of the island's thrust into the modern age: the world's largest radar-radio telescope located at the Arecibo Observatory (**these pages**). Since 1963 scientists at the Cornell University-operated facility have used the 1000-foot dish for two distinct purposes: first, as a radar, to explore both the earth's ionosphere and the surrounding solar system; and second, as a radio telescope, to "listen" to natural radio emissions originating from the far reaches of the universe.

It is, of course, the scientific aspects of the facility which give it its significance (the radar function of the observatory has made significant contributions to our understanding of the movements and structure of the Moon, Venus, and Mercury, for example, while the

As preceding sections of this book have pointed out, nothing was so significant in Puerto Rico's early history as her geographic location: the island's strategic position on the vital shipping routes in and out of the Caribbean was the dominant reason for its colonization by the Spaniards, and it was this role which determined the nature of the island's development under Spain. Again, when the U.S. invaded in 1898 and began its own role in Puerto Rico, it was the island's location—guarding the sea lanes to America's southern coast and the soon-to-be-built Panama Canal—which dominated the thinking of American strategic planners. As has been discussed, that strategic role reached its modern culmination during World War II, when the island was heavily fortified for its role in protecting the country's southeastern flank.

In today's world of missiles, long-range aircraft, and satellite surveillance, the island's importance as a strategic outpost is somewhat diminished, but military planners continue to see Puerto Rico as a vital link in the nation's defense network. The island contains a number of military installations, but none is more significant than the Roosevelt Roads Naval Station at the eastern tip of the island, the largest U.S. Navy base in the world (where a jet fighter is being refueled, **this page, upper**). The potential wartime role of the base is obvious; during peacetime the base is a key Navy training facility, with extensive electronic installations for integrated naval and air exercises.

For Commodore Diego Hernández (seen **this page, lower**, on the left, being briefed on the bridge of a visiting warship), taking up command of the U.S. Naval Forces, Caribbean, headquartered at Roosevelt Roads, meant a return to his homeland, for he is a native Puerto Rican, born and raised on the island. The Navy's selection of Commodore Hernández for this command in 1982 proved a particularly felicitous choice, for he has done much to improve the relations between the Navy and its civilian neighbors; on Vieques, especially, the island some ten miles to the east of the base, where the Navy has long conducted exercises, a particularly severe unemployment rate had helped exacerbate the civilian-military relationship. Through a series of contacts with the Viequenses initiated by the Commodore, and, as he puts it, by "being able to sit down and talk with them in their own language," the two sides were able to achieve agreement on a series of proposals—including the locating of defense subcontractors on Vieques to reduce unemployment—which promise an improved atmosphere long after the completion of the Commodore's tour of duty on the island.

Puertorricana

This is, of course, rain forest, known popularly for its dominating peak, El Yunque; officially, in the cumbersome officialese of the U.S. Forest Service, as the Caribbean National Forest, Luquillo Division. Some 1600 showers a year feed its lush vegetation, its streams, its waterfalls, including La Coca (**opposite**), surely the most photographed of all. "The only forest in the National Forest system without a forest fire problem," the brochure tells you, for this is its only tropical forest. At La Mina Falls, a half-hour hike down from the highway, the Spanish found the gold that had lured the conquistadors. When that gave out in the mid-1500s, they moved on, and the rain forest has remained little disturbed ever since.

*A*t Palmer, some 20 miles east of San Juan, you leave the main highway and enter a branch road that begins twisting up the slopes of the Sierra de Luquillo. If it is early morning, the traffic is almost non-existent, and the heavy tropical air of the coast gives way to a hint of coolness and hanging mist. You enter a world little touched by the changes of the past five centuries; indeed, little changed in eons. Ever higher: vines, trees, and giant tree ferns wall and canopy the road. The calls of wakening birds pierce the air, as do the final calls of the tiny tree frog, the coquí. The road is damp, always, for if there is no rain falling now, there was no more than a few hours ago, and the near-constant roof of clouds holds the moisture.

*I*n fact, El Yunque is the only sizeable area of the island which retains its original native vegetation. The early records indicate that the island was completely covered with forest when the Spanish arrived. The extent of the Taino population, although of course impossible to know with precision, apparently never surpassed more than about 30,000, and while they practiced some clear-and-burn agriculture, its impact on the island's aspect and total forest cover was minimal.

With the arrival of European civilization, the steady growth of the population and the advancing technology of agriculture combined to steadily remove the forest cover, as it became timber for buildings, fuel for heat, and made way for food and commercial crops. In the early years of the 19th century, forest still covered three quarters of the island, but with the great population surge of that century, by 1900 a mere 25 per cent remained as forest, and by 1950 the figure had dropped below 10 per cent. Erosion of the countryside had become a critical problem.

Then, just as demographic, economic, and technological developments were at the point of totally denuding the island, those same evolving forces brought its salvation: in the 1940s the jíbaros began their exodus from the Cordillera Central to the island's towns and cities, and then to the mainland, a tide that would grow in the '50s. The availability of gas, electricity, and concrete lifted much of the pressure from the forests as suppliers of fuel and building materials, and the decline of the island's agriculture allowed much of the higher mountain areas to return to forest.

Today roughly a quarter of the island is under forest cover; and though only El Yunque is officially considered and protected as true rain forest, in fact many of the narrow mountain valleys in the Cordillera Central have a similar vegetation and an atmosphere of dim, tree-filtered light, where the days are cool and short, hemmed in by the steep mountain slopes—and a walk under the moist forest canopy will turn up sights such as the five-inch millipede I happened upon near Dos Bocas Lake (**opposite**).

*I*t is, however, only in the unpopulated, protected reaches provided by the expanse of the El Yunque forest that the rarest of all the island's native creatures, the Puerto Rican parrot (**following pages**), is still found. *Amazona vittata*—perhaps a million of them—ranged the entire island when the Spanish arrived. Today barely 30 birds survive in the wild, with another 20 or so in a captive breeding program which hopes to increase those numbers—and the parrot's chances for survival.

High on the slopes of El Yunque I met Dr. Jim Wiley of the U.S. Fish and Wildlife Service, who is working to try to save the parrot. I joined him and his young assistant, Fernando Núñez, a biology student at the University of Puerto Rico, one day for a trek into the forest to repair some artificial nesting boxes they had placed some time before. "The chief survival problem the parrot has had has been the loss of suitable habitat—losses from natural and human predators have been a factor too, but the major cause has been the destruction of the large expanses of virgin forest the parrot needs to live and feed in. Their natural choice for nesting sites is almost always a hole in an old palo colorado tree—but there simply haven't been enough of these natural sites in the recent past to accommodate all the breeding pairs—so since the early '70s we've been building artificial nests. Here we are now." We had been slogging through the forest mud for half an hour, and had reached a forty-foot tree with a dark-green fiberglass box fastened about halfway up. I watched from a nearby blind as Jim and Fernando (**this page**, left and right, respectively) clambered up and began applying a resin patch. Some twenty minutes later, satisfied the patch would hold, we were slogging on to another site, this one a giant tree perhaps seventy feet in height. Fernando and I waited below while Jim strapped on climbing spikes and made his way to the crown of the tree alone. "The parrot almost disappeared entirely in the early '70s," Fernando commented. "The count was only 16 birds in the wild. We've made a comeback since then, but the parrot's still in a very precarious situation—and one of the rarest birds in the world. One bad hurricane could wipe out all the birds in the wild. That's why the captive breeding program was started—as insurance against total loss of the wild flock."

After three hours in the forest we headed back to the jeeps, where Fernando left us to head into Rio Piedras for his day's classes. Back at the Service's aviary, where the captive breeding program is conducted, I sat down to coffee with Jim and his wife Beth. "Our ultimate goal is to build the total flock to the point where we can reintroduce the parrot to another area of the island," Beth commented. Jim went on: "You know, as recently as the 1930s there were still around 2000 parrots here on the island—and even as late as 1954 there were over 200—if we save this species, it will have been one of the closest calls ever. But if it is to survive, one thing that will have to stop is the practice of people taking these birds from the wild and putting them in cages as pets. Ultimately, as with all preservation efforts, it is only public attitudes and awareness of the fragility of a species that can give it a chance at survival."

Photograph of Puerto Rican parrot courtesy Noel and Helen Snyder, U.S. Fish and Wildlife Service.

of greatest natural and historical interest on the island. One of the least touched and most spectacular is at the very northeastern corner of the island, the headlands and lagoons of Cabezas de San Juan (**this page, lower right**).†

Beyond the physical beauty of the site, the lagoon has recently been discovered to be "phosphorescent"—one of the rare bodies of water in the world where bioluminescent microscopic organisms called dinoflagellates exist in such numbers that the light they emit when disturbed is visible on the water's surface. (Another Trust property is famed Phosphorescent Bay on the southern coast near La Parguera, another such body of water. I toured Phosphorescent Bay twice, and on both nights I was awed by the shimmering, silvery display. That there are no photographs of that spectacular sight in this book is testimony to the fact that the human eye is an incredible instrument—one whose capabilities film and lenses are still far from equalling.)

---

† Already one of the most densely-populated places in the world, the island will likely count another million inhabitants by the year 2000—or more than 1200 people per square mile.

(Actual size of iguana about 24 inches nose to tail.)

*L*ike the parrot, the Puerto Rican iguana (**this page, upper left**) has all but vanished from the wild as a result of man's activities. Once abundant in the arid southern region of the island, the iguana was a food source for the Tainos, and considered a delicacy by the early European settlers. And, as with the parrot, the iguana has suffered even more heavily as a result of habitat loss: as population and agriculture spread into the drier areas of the island due to irrigation, the iguana's range shrank ever smaller. Today it is apparently extinct on Puerto Rico's main island, and survives in the true wild only on uninhabited Mona Island, in the passage of the same name between Puerto Rico and Hispaniola. (A colony of perhaps a hundred iguanas roam free on Isla Magueyes—where this photograph was made—a scientific preserve and research station off the southern coast.)

As the island's population continues to grow the danger is that the dwindling number of natural areas (such as this bit of coastline just north of Roosevelt Roads, **opposite**) will continue to disappear. Into the face of the enormous pressures created by this relentless growth has stepped a unique organization: the Conservation Trust of Puerto Rico. Organized in 1968, the Trust attempts to preserve, unaltered, the few remaining unspoiled sites

Despite the island's development and heavy population density, there is one bit of native fauna that has survived, and even prospered. Indeed, the tiny tree frogs popularly known as the "coquí" (ko-KEE)—actually various species of the genus Eleutherodactylus (**opposite**, shown about three times life size, is Eleutherodactylus coqui)—are so widespread throughout the island that they have become the unofficial mascot, or symbol, of Puerto Rico, and are endlessly reproduced in souvenirs and on signs (**this page**).

As any resident or visitor of the island knows, the coquí's name derives from the sound of its call. The two piercing notes are repeated endlessly throughout the night (by the males only), to attract mates and to mark territory. Most of what is known about E. coqui and the other 15 species of tree frogs found on the island has been compiled in a book by Professor Juan A. Rivero of the University of Puerto Rico's Biology Department in Mayagüez.

Professor Rivero's work indicates, for example, that only two of the tiny frog species emit a call resembling the name commonly applied to all of them. Each species has particular habitats (many of which overlap), but one or more are found virtually everywhere on the island. While it is often stated that the frogs live only in a type of plant called bromeliads, in fact various species may inhabit a great variety of plants, trees, rocks and ground litter. The great majority which I found during my efforts to photograph one for this book were an inch or less in length (some as tiny as 3/8"), but many species attain a considerably greater size—up to 3" in one mountain-dwelling type.

Another popular myth maintains that the coquí will not survive, or if it survives, will not "sing" outside Puerto Rico, but Professor Rivero dismisses such claims as nonsense, and, in fact, a singing coquí colony was recently reported in a Florida nursery, stowaways on shipments of imported tropical plants. (Related species of tree frogs are known throughout the Caribbean islands, but their nighttime calls are distinct from that of the coquí.) Paradoxically, despite their presence in nearly every corner of the island, a great many Puerto Ricans have never seen an actual coquí; they are difficult to locate by their call, since they usually cease their singing when danger is detected, and virtually impossible to locate while they sleep during the day. While I was searching for the tiny frogs outside my hotel one evening a hotel employee happened by, and when she saw a coquí "frozen" by my flashlight beam, cried in delight: "Oh, I've always loved the coquí's song, but that's the first time I've ever seen a real one!" Shy and unseen it may be, but the coquí's nighttime chorus has made it a beloved part of Borinquen.

Mi Viejo San Juan

*A*s is the case with most visitors to Puerto Rico, my first contact with the island on my first arrival some 15 years ago was with what outsiders call Old San Juan, and what Puerto Ricans call, variously, the Old City, San Juan Antiguo, Viejo San Juan, or simply, San Juan. I tend to prefer the term I have used for the title of this chapter, perhaps because it brings to mind the haunting song by the late Noel Estrada, "En Mi Viejo San Juan," which talks of the nostalgia felt by someone, like myself, who has known those narrow, cobbled, historic streets, and is far away from them.

Unlike most of those visitors, I came to know much of Puerto Rico rather well, and, as I hope the preceding pages will reflect, found it a captivating island. And yet, when all is said and done, it is that historic city within the ancient Spanish walls which remains my favorite part of Puerto Rico.

I came to know the city at all hours of the day and night, and to savor its many moods. Like many people, I have a fondness for evening there, when the day's heat, traffic, and noise fade and the street lamps lend an almost magical air to this, the oldest city under the American flag. But there are other times of the day, too, that captivate me—like late afternoon, when the slanting rays of the sun can bring golden tones to the storied balconies of Calle Fortaleza (**this page**).

*L*ike all of Puerto Rico, the city stirs to life early: the street sweepers finish their rounds, shuttered French windows on upper floor balconies swing open to let in morning's light, and people begin drifting into the plazas to read the paper, visit with friends, have a quiet smoke or perhaps a shoeshine, or—if it is the Plaza de Colón (**opposite**), wait for the bus.†

Others gather in their favorite cafeterías for the morning coffee, either negro or con leche, or a bite of breakfast. It was at my favorite haunt near the post office that I met Digno Carrillo (**this page**) one morning. He had journeyed into the city by público from Humacao, where he now lives. "I lived just a couple of blocks from here, years ago," he commented. "It's changed a lot since those days, you know. The whole country has changed, and for the better! When I was a boy, your mother gave you a piece of bread—no butter!—and you were happy to get that! Today, everyone has plenty to eat. Muñoz Marín, he was the one who changed things—a great man. He made the 'peaceful revolution' here in Puerto Rico, in the '40s." We talked on about the changes the island had seen in his lifetime, then he had to go, to keep an appointment at a government agency, one of many still found in the old city, although today many have relocated "outside the walls" as crowding in Old San Juan has become an ever greater problem. "Come and see me in Humacao," he said as he left. "I'm always with my 'bunch' in the plaza, playing dominoes. I can show you all over that part of the island."

Regrettably, I was never able to take up Señor Carrillo's offer, but I trust that he and his 'bunch' continue to enjoy the sunshine of the plaza in Humacao.

---

†A transportation project announced in 1984 should soon reroute the buses to a nearby terminal, thus ridding the plaza of its least agreeable aspect.

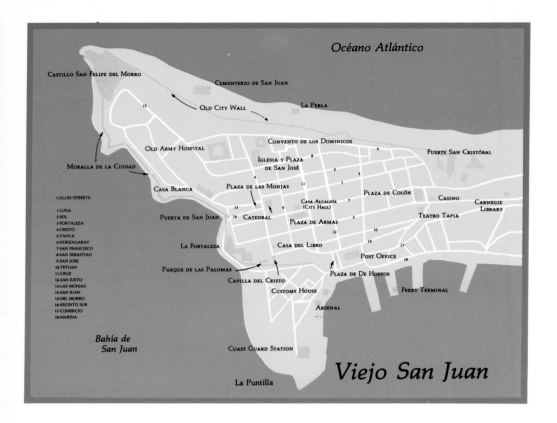

Océano Atlántico

Castillo San Felipe del Morro

Cementerio de San Juan

Old City Wall   La Perla

Muralla de la Ciudad

Old Army Hospital

Convento de los Dominicos

Fuerte San Cristóbal

Iglesia y Plaza
de San José

Casa Blanca

Plaza de las Monjas

Plaza de Colón

Puerta de San Juan

Catedral

Casa Alcaldía
(City Hall)

Plaza de Armas

Casino

Carnegie
Library

Teatro Tapia

CALLES/STREETS

1-LUNA
2-SOL
3-FORTALEZA
4-CRISTO
5-TANCA
6-NORZAGARAY
7-SAN FRANCISCO
8-SAN SEBASTIAN
9-SAN JOSE
10-TETUAN
11-CRUZ
12-SAN JUSTO
13-LAS MONJAS
14-SAN JUAN
15-DEL MORRO
16-RECINTO SUR
17-COMERCIO
18-MARINA

La Fortaleza

Casa del Libro

Parque de las Palomas

Capilla del Cristo

Post Office

Plaza de De Hostos

Customs House

Ferry Terminal

Arsenal

Bahía de
San Juan

Coast Guard Station

La Puntilla

Viejo San Juan

For many who live on the opposite side of the bay, the Cataño ferry (**opposite**) provides the chance to avoid the traffic, and at a fare of ten cents is doubtless the greatest bargain in Puerto Rico. Early morning runs are full of secretaries and other workers bound for their jobs in Old San Juan, chatting, reading the paper, putting finishing touches on make-up, or catching a few more minutes' sleep before starting the work day. On arrival, true to Latin style, a chivalrous deck-hand offers the ladies a helping hand onto the dock (**this page, lower right**).

Only a few blocks square, and laid out long before the automobile arrived on the scene, the blue-bricked streets are a walker's paradise with nearly five centuries of history in a microcosm. (Indeed, the coming of the automobile in large numbers has wrought havoc with the city's atmosphere—in both the figurative and literal senses—and the near-constant traffic jam on the old city's main arteries is probably the most disagreeable side of its nature. At this writing, a plan—not without opposition—was in progress to remove traffic from the main "loop" through the city, substituting motorized trolleys in the place of cars, and converting the streets into pedestrian malls.)

As has been discussed (**see** "Beginnings"), it was San Juan's bay that was vital to Spain's control of her trade routes, so it was logical to locate the city near "El Morro," the headland overlooking the harbor mouth. To ensure dominance of that strategic entrance, the Crown in 1539 authorized construction of the first fortifications on the site.

Enlargements and improvements would continue over the next two and a half centuries; major construction on the fort as we see it today (in an aerial view, **opposite**, and an interior shot, **this page**) rising to a total height of 140 feet above the water line, began in 1591. The fort took on the name Castillo de San Felipe del Morro, for the Spanish king, Philip II. But El Morro alone proved to be inadequate to prevent successful sieges and occupations of the city, first by the English under the Earl of Cumberland in 1598, then by the Dutch in 1625 (who sacked and burned the city before departing). These attacks, and the new proximity of the English, Dutch and French who were establishing their own colonies in the Lesser Antilles, led the Spanish authorities to begin further fortifications at strategic points for the defense of the city (including Fort San Cristóbal and the massive stone walls which would eventually surround the city, both begun about 1634). The value and strength of these fortifications would prove themselves in 1797, when the English made one last (and unsuccessful) attack on the city.

Then, as the 19th century unfolded, Spain lost her New World colonies to revolutionary movements, and pirate raids became but a dim memory. The original need for El Morro evaporated, and for a century her guns were silent. Not until 1898, with the Spanish-American War, would San Juan again come under attack, but, as has so often been the case in Puerto Rico's history, the outcome of that conflict would be determined far from the island's shores, and on October 18 of that year, El Morro and the rest of the island would be turned over to the American forces by virtue of a treaty signed in Paris.†

---

†The Treaty of Paris did not end El Morro's active military life, however; both it and San Cristóbal were actively manned during World War II, and continued to house U.S. military units into the 1960s.

*I*t is of course the buildings within the walls which give Viejo San Juan its special atmosphere. While many are of relatively recent vintage (certainly the great majority dating from this and the second half of the 19th centuries; see **following two pages** for a smattering of the finer and more interesting examples), others have a much older history. Two of the most important and imposing are those shown here: the Casa Alcaldía, or City Hall, of San Juan (**this page**) has stood on its present site facing the Plaza de Armas since about 1604 (the building has been much added to and remodeled over the years; the present façade dates from the 1840s).

Just a block away, on Calle Cristo, stands the Catedral de San Juan Bautista (**opposite**), probably the most famous of all buildings within the city walls, and the site where the tomb of the colony's founder, Juan Ponce de León, is located. The first church on the site dates from 1521, and thus the Cathedral rightly claims the honor of being the oldest church on the island. The original rustic church was destroyed by hurricane in 1539, however; it was rebuilt the following year, and underwent many modifications over the next century and a half. The bulk of the present structure was erected in the first half of the 19th century. Thus it is that the Church of San José (**see** "Beginnings"), at the top of Cristo Street a couple of blocks away, the core of which dates from the 1530s, rightly claims to be the oldest church (building) in Puerto Rico (and, in fact, the second oldest in the New World—being antedated only by the Cathedral of Santo Domingo, in the neighboring Dominican Republic, whose construction dates from 1521).

battle with motorists unable to find legal parking places, are subjected to various explanations for their victims' transgressions (**opposite, lower left**—this one got off).

Yet another traditional and beloved feature of the island's popular culture are the piragüeros and their pushcarts. Alberto Aviles Ortiz has manned his cart in the Plaza de Armas (**opposite, upper right**) for the last 55 of his 77 years, and offers 13 flavors of snowcones—or any combination thereof.

Mobile food stands are everywhere a part of the Puerto Rican landscape, especially along the main roads leading out of the San Juan. Here (**opposite, lower right**), a traveling plantain seller sets up shop from the back of his station wagon on one of the streets of the old city.

*B*eyond its colorful and historic architecture, it is the constant and varied activity of its streets and plazas that give the city its vitality and charm. Lottery salesmen like the one pictured (**this page, upper left**) at his usual spot on Calle San Francisco have been a feature of the island since a lottery was first instituted in 1812. A newer feature are sidewalk painters, like the one who frequents the Parque de las Monjas in front of the Cathedral (**this page, lower right**) recording in quick oils, for tourists, mainly, the architecture of the city.

The domino games at La Barandilla (**opposite page, upper left**), as the park at the corner of Calle San Francisco and Calle Tanca is commonly known, are a continuous feature from early morning to dark, as they are in the central plazas of towns throughout the island. The beleaguered municipal police, caught up in a constant

to sell their beautifully-mounted butterfly displays—some of which combine to form wall-size murals valued in the thousands of dollars—is without doubt the most unusual business in Viejo San Juan.

The narrow streets are lined with restaurants, gift and jewelry shops, and art galleries (**this page, lower right**), and occasionally, full of shops as well, when an open-air crafts fair is set up in the Callejón de la Capilla to give island artisans a chance to market their creations.

Stone and bronze plaques dot the walls of the old city, noting historical events which occurred in one building or another (one claims the honor of having been the site where the island's most popular drink, the piña colada—a mixture of coconut milk, pineapple juice, and rum—was invented; another, of special in-

*I*t is hardly surprising that this combination of Old World architecture and the liveliness and intimacy of the streets has made Old San Juan a favorite place for artists of all kinds, from the itinerant sidewalk painter to the most renowned and established artists like Rafael Tufiño, Jan D'Esopo and Carlos Irizarry. The same combination of elements has made the old city a favorite area among the sizeable community of "continentals" (mainland-born Americans) who have adopted Puerto Rico as their home. Of these, perhaps none is better known than Drakir Purington (**this page, upper left**) who first came to the island in the fifties, and, with his wife, began an itinerant business of selling displays of butterflies mounted in clear plastic boxes. Today their "Butterfly People" on Calle Fortaleza, where they continue

terest to me, notes that the Spanish priest, Fray Junípero Serra stayed there in 1749, en route to Mexico, where he would later found the missions of California).

And of course what makes Viejo San Juan particularly fascinating is the fact that it is a living, breathing, working city, where you encounter all manner of people, including the young lady (**this page, upper right**) whom I saw one day waiting for her mother in the Plaza de Armas.

With such an intermingling of human and historical elements, it is hardly surprising that the old city has become the island's major tourist attraction. In the winter months, especially, the streets are full of tourists from colder climes, many of whom will be boarding one of the cruise ships which have made San Juan their

home port for winter cruises (**this page, lower left**, a cruise ship overnights at a pier near the post office building).

The city has such an air of permanency to it that it is difficult to imagine that it ever looked otherwise—and yet the fact remains that visitors to Old San Juan only thirty years ago came away with a very different impression. As the capital's growing population expanded beyond its walled confines around the turn of the century, the classic pattern of central-city decline set in, with commerce, housing, and business gravitating toward the newer, "nicer" part of town. Property values "within the walls" declined, maintenance and refurbishing were neglected, and the old city began taking on the aspect of a dilapidated, inner-city slum.

That Old San Juan was rescued from its sad decay to become the living museum it is today, delight for both tourist and resident alike, was largely the work of two inspired men. One of them was that giant of modern Puerto Rico already discussed, Luis Muñoz Marín, who guided the island into its modern industrial era with Operation Bootstrap. But Muñoz realized that the transformation of an economy inevitably threatens the cultural underpinnings of a society, and in 1955 he launched "Operation Serenity" as a companion—or counterbalance—to the industrialization program. Its mission was to preserve and promote the island's cultural heritage.

As is usually the case with great leaders, part of Muñoz's genius lay in finding and appointing people ideally suited to the organizations they were to direct: in 1955 he demonstrated that genius once again by naming a young archeologist, Ricardo Alegría, to be the first director of the Institute of Puerto Rican Culture, the organization that would spearhead Operacíon Serenidad (the Institute today has its headquarters and conducts many of its programs in the 16th-century Convento de los Dominicos, **opposite,** *among the finest restorations on the island). Dr. Alegría had already made a name for himself while still a doctoral candidate at Harvard with his discoveries relating to the Taino culture in Puerto Rico, most notably the unearthing and restoration of the ceremonial ball courts near Utuado. But it would be his 18-year tenure as head of the Instituto, and its outstanding achievement in transforming Viejo San Juan which brought him to prominence not only at home, but far from Puerto Rico's shores as well.*

I joined Dr. Alegría (seen **this page,** *on the right, talking with a friend on Calle San Juan) for a walking tour of the city one October morning. His pride was evident, as would be expected, as he pointed out the various buildings that had been saved through the efforts of the Institute and private citizens (the Commonwealth government stimulated private efforts with a combination of low interest loans and tax incentives). But there was a surprising note of discouragement as well. "Actually, the city was at its peak a few years ago, maybe shortly after the time you first came to Puerto Rico in 1969. There's been a terrible relaxation of standards in the past few years—in an attempt to lure the tourist, I suppose. See those banners, those signs hanging from those shops? They would never have been allowed some years back.*

People can be so short-sighted. You may lure another tourist or two into your own shop with those things, but what about the overall effect? In the long run, you'll lose thousands of tourists who will never come to the island at all, if the city begins to look like a carnival ground. There are already plenty of 'tourist traps' in the Caribbean—we don't need to be another. And what about the people, like me, who call Viejo San Juan home? All our restoration efforts were, in the final analysis, aimed at restoring the authenticity—and the dignity—of this city. I can only hope that people will come to their senses and realize that that is what makes this old city distinctive, and fascinating, both for tourists and for those of us who live here."

*T*he lament Dr. Alegría had voiced stayed with me for a long time, and I suppose his words were on my mind when I went down to the San Juan Gate one evening shortly before I completed the photography for this book and prepared to leave the island. I had gone down to the water's edge for one last try at a sunset picture; alas, the western sky was overcast, and there would be no colors to compare with those which had silhouetted the sentry box and city wall some months before **(opposite)**. So I just sat on the sea wall with my thoughts for a while, reflecting on the past few months I had spent on the island.

Soon the city's street lamps came flickering on, as twilight crept in, and then a container ship full of merchandise from the mainland slipped quietly into the harbor, past silent El Morro and the city walls. Here, in the falling darkness, were juxtaposed the island's past and its present. Here was symbolized the struggle to preserve Puerto Rico's centuries of heritage and at the same time move forward to enable all its people to enjoy the fruits of the modern age. History, especially that of the past century, has shown that only the people of Puerto Rico can mold these often-conflicting elements into a harmonious whole; with hard work, love for their country, and Si Dios quiere—"God willing"--as they are fond of saying, they will continue to do so.

Acknowledgements

Having been a reader far longer than a writer, I know that this is a section often given little notice by most readers. It should not be so, at least with a book of this nature, for it owes a great deal to the generous cooperation of an untold number of people. The contribution of many of these individuals and organizations will be apparent from the text or from the credit lines at the photographs themselves, and I would like to express my gratitude to them, and also, in Puerto Rico, to:

The Office of the Governor of Puerto Rico
Señora Kate D. de Romero
Teodoro Vidal
Priamo and Shirley Pichardo
Tom Marvel
Sister Leticia (Utuado)
Institute of Puerto Rican Culture
Conservation Trust of Puerto Rico
General Archives of Puerto Rico
National Park Service
Library of Congress
Galería Botello
Museum of the University of Puerto Rico
Department of Biology of the University of Puerto Rico (Isla Magueyes)
McAllister Brothers Inc.
Sea-Land Services Inc.
and to Walter Murray Chiesa, Director of Fomento's Office of Crafts Development, who lent his time, encouragement, and guidance to this project, becoming in the process a valued friend. Without his enthusiastic support this book would be far less than it is;

and, in California, to:

Tim Sweeney, for reviewing and commenting on the English text
Marie LaBrucherie, for secretarial assistance
Quentin Burke, for advice on printing details
Amparo and Mónica Guajardo Maldonado, of Mexicali, Mexico, for laboring so hard on the Spanish translation
and, finally, to Martha, whose love through the years has been the unseen support for many, many images.

Corporate Sponsors

Production of a book of this nature inevitably means the assistance of countless individuals and organizations, both public and private. Among the most valued supporters of this project have been the following corporate sponsors, without whose participation this book would never have come into being. It should perhaps be pointed out that, while each of these sponsors has been generous with financial support, none has either sought or been accorded prior review of the content of this book. The opinions expressed are therefore solely those of the author, and he alone is responsible for any errors or omissions which may have escaped notice.

Underwriters

Arthur Andersen & Co.
Banco Central Corp.
Bank of Boston
Capacete, Martín & Associates
Caribe Hilton International
Cerromar Beach Hotel
Condado Plaza Hotel & Casino

Howard Johnson's Nabori Lodge
Levitt Homes Incorporated
Mazda de Puerto Rico
Méndez & Co. Inc.
Nestlé-Libby (Puerto Rico), Inc.
The SmithKline Beckman Companies
Yabucoa Sun Oil Co.

Contributors

Abbott Laboratories
Able Sales Co., Inc.
Alcon (Puerto Rico), Inc.
The Allen Group Puerto Rico Inc.
Burroughs
Cancio, Nadal & Rivera
Central Soya Puerto Rico, Inc.
Cervecería India, Inc.
Converse de Puerto Rico, Inc.
Daniel Contruction Company International
Eastern Airlines
GTE Sylvania Special Products
Information Magnetics Caribe, Inc.
Intership

ITT All America Cables and Radio, Inc.
Johnson & Johnson Baby Products Co.
Kodak Caribbean, Ltd.
Matsushita Electric of Puerto Rico, Inc.
Medtronic Puerto Rico, Inc.
Nabisco Brands Inc. - Puerto Rico Branch
National Can Puerto Rico, Inc.
Ochoa Industrial Sales Corp.
Olympic Mills Corp.
Peat, Marwick, Mitchell & Co.
The Shell Company (Puerto Rico) Limited
Star-Kist Caribe, Inc.
To-Ricos, Inc.
Torres, Beauchamp, Marvel y Asociados

Notes

Images of Puerto Rico is not, nor does it pretend to be, an in-depth analysis of Puerto Rican history, culture, or society. It is, rather, essentially a collection of impressions, both verbal and visual, of the island; for those seeking more detailed treatment, there are a number of writers, far better positioned than I, who have published numerous such studies. Among them are Arturo Morales Carrión and Kal Wagenheim, just two of the authors on whose works I have relied extensively in preparing this volume. Other sources utilized were virtually all of the Puerto Rican newspapers during my stay on the island, as well as the standard reference sources. As will be readily apparent from a reading of the text, much of it is based on personal observation and conversations during the time I have spent on the island.

Walter Murray Chiesa was kind enough to review and comment on the English text, and José J. Villamil generously rendered the same service for the Spanish version. I have incorporated many (though not all) of their observations; to both I am deeply indebted, and this work is the better for their contributions. Naturally, it is the author alone who bears final responsibility for the accuracy and content of this book.

The late-afternoon sun burnishes the *adoquines* of the Old City.

Photographic Notes

Most of the photographs for Images of Puerto Rico were shot during a period of five months in late 1983 and early 1984. My principal films were Kodachrome 64 and 25, with a few shots on Ektachrome 400; I have, over the years worked with a number of color films, but for overall quality of both the filmstock and processing, I have yet to find films to match Kodak's. (When shooting for reproduction tranparency films are generally superior to print films.) I worked with Nikon equipment, as I have for the past twelve years, because, while I feel that there are a number of excellent camera systems, I have found Nikon bodies and lenses unmatched for ruggedness and reliability, an important consideration when shooting on location.

I worked with three camera bodies (a Nikon F3 and two Nikon FE's), although I usually carried only two at any one time. Additional bodies facilitate using different films and are essential "back-ups." I used ten different Nikkor lenses, varying in focal length from 15mm to 500mm; along with many other photographers, I find the Nikkor 105mm to be superb for portraiture as well as a great deal of general shooting; my 24mm and 80-200 zoom lenses also saw a lot of use.

I am often asked what differentiates an amateur from a professional photographer; there are of course a number of factors, of which equipment is one. But to my mind the essential difference can be summarized as follows: an amateur takes pictures, while a professional makes pictures. By this I mean that any photograph a professional expects to publish is usually the end result of a fairly involved process which begins with an idea, or concept, and is followed by planning and preparation. The eventual snapping of the shutter is often a fairly small part of the whole process. It may of course mean going back repeatedly to redo a shot (especially where nature is involved) until it comes out as the photographer hoped or envisioned: I probably made photographs of sunsets from the Puerta de San Juan on at least a dozen different evenings before I got the shot that became the cover of this book; and during the months I spent photographing the island, I logged over 17,000 miles over its roads and highways. And of course as a general matter in publishing photographs it never hurts to have a large number of shots from which to select: the photographs appearing in this book, for example, were chosen from over 9,000 of my original transparencies.

Auselio Rivera, age 6, smiles into the camera near Maunabo.

Posed before Ponce's famed, historic firehouse is author-photographer Roger LaBrucherie. Mr. LaBrucherie received his education at Harvard College and Stanford University, taking degrees in economics and law from the latter. His first contact with the Caribbean came in the early 1970s during his service in the U.S. Peace Corps, when he trained and served in Puerto Rico and the Dominican Republic, respectively. His first book, *Imágenes de Santo Domingo*, grew out of his five years in the latter country; since then he has published three other photographic-essay books in addition to the present volume: *Images of Barbados*, *Images of Bermuda*, and *A Barbados Journey*. He makes his home in his native California.

Standing in Ponce's central plaza, the striking red-and-black *Parque de Bombas* was built shortly after the fire department's founding in 1883 (the date commemorated on the building itself), as an exhibition hall for a church celebration. After the festivities the building was put to use as a firehouse, a function it continues to serve to this day. (A modern firehouse down the street supplements the structure.)

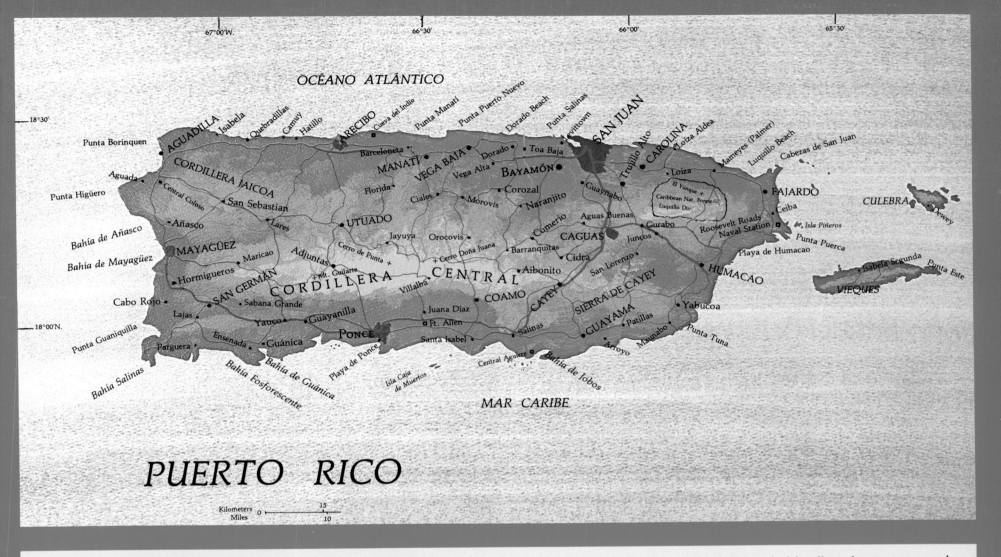

OCÉANO ATLÁNTICO

PUERTO RICO

MAR CARIBE

Kilometers
Miles
0   15
           10

Location and geography: smallest and easternmost of the Greater Antilles, Puerto Rico lies between the island of Hispaniola, 75 miles to the west across the Mona Passage, and the Virgin Islands, some 40 miles to the east. The island is about 1600 miles southeast of New York, 1000 miles from Miami, and 500 miles north of Caracas, Venezuela. The island measures approximately 110 miles east to west, and 35 miles north to south. Total area: 3435 square miles (8897 square kilometers), including its adjacent islands, of which Vieques, Culebra and Mona are the largest. The interior of the island presents a rugged mountainous aspect, which characterizes about three fourths of its area; the dominant range, with elevations above 3,000 feet, is the Cordillera Central, running east to west somewhat to the south of the center of the island. Highest island elevation: 4389 feet (1338 meters) at Cerro de Punta.

Population: (1984, est.) 3,300,000 inhabitants. Population density about 1000 persons per square mile. *Major municipalities and their populations:* San Juan (capital)—435,000; Bayamón—196,000; Ponce—190,000; Carolina—166,000; Caguas—88,000; Mayagüez—85,000.

Government: since 1952, a commonwealth in voluntary association with the United States; officially, the Commonwealth of Puerto Rico, or *Estado Libre Asociado de Puerto Rico* ("Free Associated State of Puerto Rico"), in Spanish. Essentially self-governing under the Constitution of Puerto Rico in all internal matters, although federal law governs in many areas (including the cur-

rency, post office, customs and immigration). Universal adult suffrage elects a governor and a bicameral legislature; the judiciary completes the tripartite governmental structure. Puerto Ricans are U.S. citizens, with all the incumbent rights and obligations; U.S. citizens resident in Puerto Rico have no vote in federal elections and do not pay federal tax on island-generated income.

Economy: based principally on manufacturing (pharmaceuticals, electronics, clothing, textiles, etc.), which in 1955 surpassed agriculture as the primary economic sector. Tourism is second in economic importance; agriculture (mainly dairying, beef cattle and sugar cane) is now a distant third. Per capita income (1981): $3500.

Climate: tropical; along the north coast mean temperature varies from 80°F (27°C.) in summer to 75°F. (24°C.) in winter, with about 60″ (1500mm) of rainfall distributed fairly evenly throughout the year, heaviest May—December. The south coast is considerably drier and somewhat warmer; the mountainous interior, considerably cooler. Temperatures are moderated by the near-constant northeasterly trade winds.

Miscelaneous: *Language:* Spanish; English widely spoken. *Religion:* predominantly Roman Catholic, significant minority of Protestant adherents; complete freedom of religion and separation of church and state.

Imágenes Press
P.O. Box 653
El Centro, California 92244 USA
Tel: (619) 352-2188

Printed in China

Images of Puerto Rico
ISBN 0-939302-09-8 (Standard Laminated Edition)
ISBN 0-939302-10-1 (Deluxe Clothbound Edition)
ISBN 0-939302-11-X (Boxed Collector's Edition)

Also available in a Spanish-language edition:
Imágenes de Puerto Rico

Typeset in Paladium Italic at the facilities of the
Holtville Tribune, Holtville, California

Second printing

A bronze door knocker in Viejo San Juan.